Designer Desserts

Prestige des Grands Chefs

Designer Desserts

by
Philippe Durand

under the direction of
Pierre Michalet
Translated by Anne Sterling

A copublication of

cicem

and

WILEY

Author
Philippe DURAND

Philippe Durand was born in 1957 in Dinard, Brittany. His parents and grandparents owned a pastry shop in Lancieux.

At 16, he began his apprenticeship in Dinan in the pastry shop of well known chef Gautier who was then president of the «Chambre de Métiers» of Côtes d'Amor. After obtaining his CAP Patissier, Confiseur, Chocolatier, Glacier (culinary aptitude certification in all branches of pastry), he served in the military then went to Paris to gain experience in top pastry kitchens. In Switzerland, under the tutelage of Chef Angerhn, he developed an interest in chocolate work, a field in which he has excelled.

Philippe Durand then returned to take charge of the family pastry shop and to continue his education, earning the «Brevet de Maîtrise Patissier, Confiseur, Glacier». In 1986, he began teaching at the Lycée Louis Guilloux in Rennes. He specialized in chocolate and candy and also developed a special course in «designer desserts» for restaurant service.

During this time, Philippe Durand participated in several culinary competitions and won the following awards:

• Arpajon: First Prize in Chocolate, 1990 and 1991
• Romorantin: First prize Desserts, 1990
• Nantes: First prize Chocolate, 1990
• STLO Competition: First prize, Chocolate 1990
• Paris (Intersuc Competition):
Finalist: «Grand Prix International du Chocolat», 1990, 1992, 1994
First Prize: Dégustation, 1990

Chef Durand has worked diligently to develop his ideas for the classroom so that future chefs will learn the techniques and creativity needed to arrange and decorate elaborate individual desserts.

The «Lycée Louis Guilloux in Rennes»: An ideal atmosphere for the creation of this book

Many thanks to the directors, staff and students of this school and for the use of their outstanding facility which made the preparation of the desserts in this book possible.

CONFÉDÉRATION NATIONALE
DE LA
PÂTISSERIE-CONFISERIE-CHOCOLATERIE-GLACERIE
DE FRANCE

Dans le cadre de mes responsabilités confédérales, j'ai la chance
d'oeuvrer à la promotion de mon métier par la formation.

Je suis, en effet, convaincu que la pâtisserie artisanale est beaucoup plus
qu'une activité. C'est une réelle passion qui s'entretient par le développement
des connaissances et la création esthétique.

Or, comment mieux s'y consacrer sinon en pratiquant des techniques
particulières comme notamment celles des desserts à l'assiette ? On y révèle non
seulement ses capacités professionnelles, mais aussi ses qualités artistiques.

Reste, cependant, à bien choisir ses références, c'est-à-dire à approcher
les meilleurs Maîtres qui dominent leur art et savent le dispenser.

C'est ce que permet la lecture du présent ouvrage où Philippe DURAND
fait partager avec ferveur et pédagogie les multiples facettes de son talent.

Merci donc à ce grand artiste et merci aussi aux Editions Saint-Honoré
de mettre à la disposition de tous les professionnels cette formidable leçon.

François CARTON

4, rue de Hanovre 75002 PARIS · Téléphone : (1) 47 42 41 57 · Télécopie : (1) 47 42 53 04
Préfecture de Paris N° 1524

Among my responsibilities as vice president of the Pastry Confederation is to promote the advancement of my profession through education. I am convinced that pastry making is more than a job. It is a passion which is expressed through creativity and the mastery of techniques.

And how better to show our skills than in the execution of «designer desserts»? By creating stunning individual desserts, each of us can express ourselves as chef and artist.

To learn these skills, we must look to the masters who have dedicated themselves to their art and know how to teach it to others.

In this book, Philippe Durand has enthusiastically shared his knowledge. Many thanks to this great artist and to «Editions St-Honoré» for creating a valuable teaching tool for professional and amateur cooks. **François CARTON**

• Président des Patissiers de Bretagne
• Président de la Commission de la Formation de la Confédération Nationale de la Pâtisserie, Confiserie, Chocolaterie, Glacerie de France
• Vice Président de la Confédération Nationale de la Pâtisserie, Confiserie, Chocolaterie, Glacerie de France

CONTENTS

The editor and author of «**Designer Desserts**» have organized the information in a format that makes the book simple to use.

Chapter 1

The principles and techniques for «designer desserts» are outlined in this chapter with words and pictures. The various elements of decoration are also explained: decorations with fruits, chocolate, cooked sugar, sauces and glazes, cookies and other decorations.
Basic pastry techniques are explained and shown in pictures.

Chapters 2-5

The main part of the book presents a hundred «designer desserts» with formulas and photographs. The reader will learn step by step to choose and organize the ingredients and decorations and how to arrange each dessert on the individual plates.
To make this book easy to use, the desserts are grouped according to a main ingredient: fruits, chocolate, coffee, various flavorings, etc.
These «designer desserts» can serve two purposes for the reader:
*The novice chef can follow the directions step by step and recreate the desserts as described and pictured.
*The «idea» of each dessert can inspire a more skilled cook to create his or her own variation.

Chapter 6

In this chapter each dessert is outlined to show degree of difficulty, food cost, decorations and preparation time.
To round out this chapter are the 70 basic recipes used to make the desserts in this book. This will serve as a useful reference for making any dessert.

Table of Contents

Chapitre 1 - Techniques and Methods for "Designer" Desserts

"Eye Appeal" - An Added Dimension

The moment has finally arrived to have dessert, why not make it a feast for the eyes as well as the palate?!

In a restaurant or at home, the visual effect of food plays a key role in how much the dessert is enjoyed.

Outlined here are techniques and methods, along with examples, for mastering this all important part of fine dining.

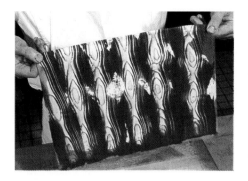

Plate presentation (as opposed to "table service" and the "dessert cart") has become very popular in French restaurants over the last few decades and has many advantages for the chef.

In response to this trend, new styles of plates are introduced each year with interesting shapes, colors and decorations to inspire and tempt the chef to try new presentations.

This has opened a whole new world of expression for the chef.

1. Personalize your presentation: The plate is your canvas to express your creative side. The rim is the frame of your picture.

2. Special decorations can be created for clients on special occasions: birthdays, anniversaries, company celebrations.

3. By creating the final presentation of the dish in the kitchen, the chef can now oversee the preparation from conception to service.

4. The kitchen can better organize the preparation and control the quality.

5. Food costs can be better controlled when desserts are sold "à la carte" or ordered from the menu, rather than served in small pieces from a dessert cart.

6. When desserts are arranged on plates, there is less waste and each dessert is absolutely fresh.

Basic Principles for Arranging Food on a Plate

How to choose a plate?

This is a difficult question to answer because it depends so much on personal taste.

It is not practical to have different plates especially chosen for each dessert. With a small selection, desserts can be paired with a plate that harmonizes with the colors and shapes of the dessert without distracting from it.

Themes to Consider

Color Harmony:

- Analogous : The same color in several different tones or colors close on the color wheel (yellow and orange, for example) are used for an overall effect. Select dessert ingredients, garnishes and plates that play on this color theme.

- Monochrome: A single color dominates and elements in the dessert match colors in the plate. It is difficult to make this color theme work.

- Polychrome: Use many colors to give a feeling of freshness and movement.

Coordinating the Plate and the Dessert

- Shape: Use plates of different shapes to tie in with the forms found in the dessert itself. Molds in various shapes, to makes mousses and layered cakes, can be purchased to match the shape of special plates.

- Material: The material used to make a plate can enhance the elements of the dessert. Earthenware is the right choice for a rustic dessert while porcelain should be used for refined, sophisticated preparations.

- Motif: A decoration on the plate, a fruit for example, can match a fruit used in the dessert.

- Desserts can be presented on a "dessert" plate, a "regular" dinner plate or an oversized presentation plate. Match the size and volume of the dessert to the size of the plate.

Advice

- A plate with too much detail can only be used for relatively plain desserts and is therefore not as versatile.

- A plain white plate, with not even a relief pattern, may seem dull on the one hand, but offers "carte blanche" to the creator to use color, shape and texture to make a statement.

- A clear plate gives a cold impression and is not recommended.

Each cook should express his or her own taste through presentation.

Methods for Plate Presentation

Series A

Example: Charlotte of Fresh Fruits
(page 38)

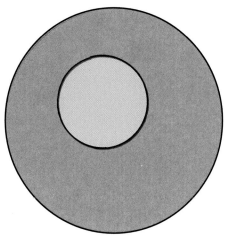

A1 - Place the charlotte off center.

A2 - Mound the fruits in a free form arrangement rather than placing them in a pattern.

A3 - Spoon just a little coulis on the other side of the plate.

Series B

Example: "Croustillants" with Red Fruits
(page 45)

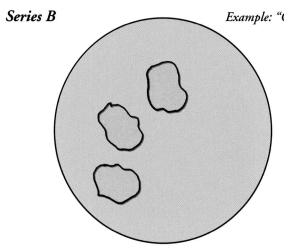

B1 - Use two spoons to place neat, oval-shaped "quenelles" of cream on one side of the plate.

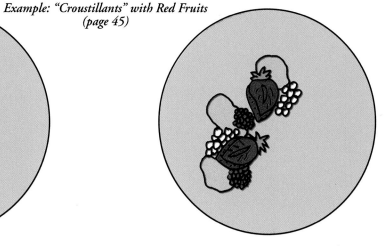

B2 - Place the fruits in a pretty arrangement on the whipped cream.

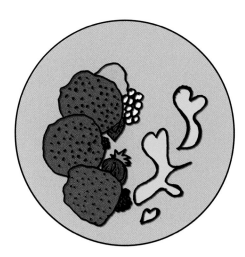

B3 - Prop the "croustillants" against the cream "quenelles" at an angle to give height to the dessert. Spoon just enough sauce on the other side of the plate.

Examples of "Designer" Desserts

1. Raspberry Dome *(page 46)*
First cover the bottom of the plate with a thin layer of sabayon, then place the dessert in the center.
The decoration for this dessert is simply the careful placement of the raspberries in a circle around the dome, which contrast with the sabayon. This is an easy presentation.

2. Coffee Charlotte with Apricot Coulis *(page 133)*
The charlotte is placed off center and the sauces are piped on the other side of the plate with a paper cone. The fruits are arranged in a curve, following the form of the plate. The round shapes give a "soft" impression.

3. Banana Dome *(page 96)*
The dome itself is quite plain which shows off the fancy chocolate decoration. The sauce is applied with a paper cone to compliment the lines of the decoration. The garnishes, cigarette cookies and chocolate disk, give some height to this pure, stylized presentation.

4. Tropical Fruit Sorbet *(page 92)*
The baked filo decorations alternate with the scoops of sorbet to break up the monotony of shapes. The colorful fruits are placed in a natural pattern, like a basket of fruit, to give the impression of the abundance one might find on a tropical island. The sauce is placed off to the side to avoid symmetry.

5. Mint Granité in a Choclate cup *(page 155)*
The choclate cup is placed in the center and the sauce is spooned in a neat circle around without overflowing to the rim. Since the dessert is in the center, the fruit garnish is arranged in a symmetrical pattern. The decorative chocolate cup is enough decoration and the dark color contrasts well with the white plate.

6. Chocolate Leaves with Mousse and Hazelnut Meringue *(page 126)*
The leaves are placed to one side and the sauce is spooned on the other. The cigarettes and cocoa powder offset the presentation. The dessert is made of two elements which should become one in the final presention.

Decorating with Fruits - *A - Sliced Fruits*

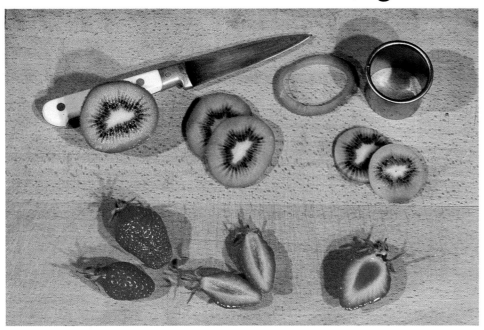

Strawberries
Wash strawberries in cold water and pat dry. Cut them in half form the stem to the point, leaving a bit of stem on each side. Brush the surface with melted red currant jelly to make it shine.

Kiwis
Choose firm (not hard) fruits. Cut into 3 mm (1/8 in) slices, trim the skin and make perfect rounds with a small cookie cutter.

Mango
Choose a mango that is perfectly ripe and cut away the skin with a paring knife. Cut from the stem end to the bottom, on either side of the flat seed to remove the two "cheeks". Cut the fruit into strips.

Star Fruit
Rinse and slice thinly (2 mm (1/12 in)).

Peaches

Peel peaches by plunging them in boiling water a few seconds and removing the loosened skin. Cut four sections and pull out the stone. Cut the quarters into slices.

Oranges

Cut away the peel (with the pith) to expose the juicy flesh of the orange. Cut on either side of each section to remove it from the membranes.

Grapes

Clean grapes in cold water. Use a small paring knife to peel the skin down from the stem end.

Passion Fruit

Clean the fruits and cut in half. (The cut fruit makes a pretty decoration, the diner will scoop out the seeds and leave the skin.)

B - Poached fruits

Pears

Peel pears and rub with lemon to keep them from discoloring. Immerse them in simmering syrup and poach 15 minutes or until the point of a paring knife penetrates easily. Cool in the syrup. Cut the pears in quarters and remove the stem and the core,

Poaching syrup: 1 L (1 qt) water, 1 kg (2 lbs) sugar, juice of 1 lemon, 1 vanilla bean

Lemons/Oranges

Rinse the fruit. Make channel cuts at even intervals and cut into thin slices (2 mm (1 1/2 in)). Arrange the slices in a single layer, pour boiling syrup over them and leave to cool in the syrup. Store in the syrup until ready to use.

Poaching syrup: 1 L (1 qt) water, 1.2 kg (2 lbs 7 oz) sugar

C - Baked fuits

Apples/Bananas

Peel the fruits. Cut the apples into wedges and remove the core. Cut the bananas in half lengthwise. Brush a baking dish with melted butter. Arrange the apples or bananas in a single layer and brush melted butter on the fruits. Sprinkle the fruits with sugar and bake at 200 C (400 F) for 15 minutes.
Flame the baked apples with Calvados and the baked bananas with rum.

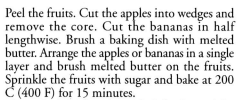

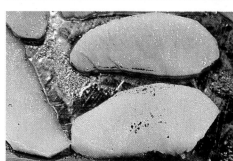

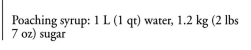

D - Lightly candied fruits

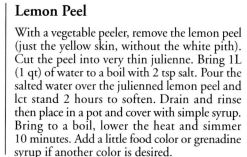

Pineapple

Drain the syrup from a #10 can of pineapple slices. Bring the syrup to a boil with 450 g (scant 1 lb) of sugar and one vanilla bean, split and scraped. Arrange the pineapple slices in a single layer and cover with boiling syrup, let cool completely in the syrup. Pour off the liquid, bring back to a boil and repeat the process. Repeat the whole procedure a third time, then store the candied fruit in the syrup in the refrigerator.

Lemon Peel

With a vegetable peeler, remove the lemon peel (just the yellow skin, without the white pith). Cut the peel into very thin julienne. Bring 1L (1 qt) of water to a boil with 2 tsp salt. Pour the salted water over the julienned lemon peel and lct stand 2 hours to soften. Drain and rinse then place in a pot and cover with simple syrup. Bring to a boil, lower the heat and simmer 10 minutes. Add a little food color or grenadine syrup if another color is desired.

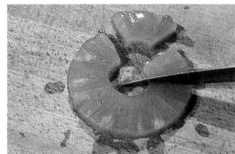

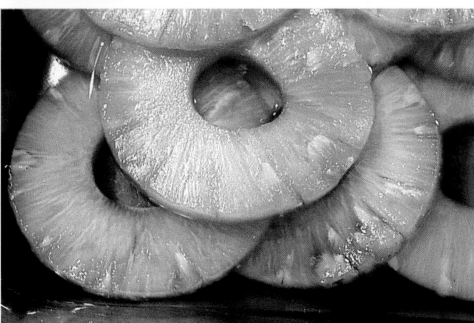

15

E - Caramelized fruits

Apricots

Drain canned apricots (they should be firm, not mushy). Dry on paper towels to absorb excess syrup.

Dip the cut side of each apricot in sugar to coat completely. Arrange the apricots in a single layer in a baking dish, sugar side up. Caramelize the sugar under the broiler or with a special French caramelizing "salamander".

F - Macerated fruits

Nuts

Make a syrup with 30 ml (1 fl oz) water and 100 g (3 1/2 oz) sugar and cook to 110 C (215 F). Add 100 g (3 1/2 oz) nuts (blanched almonds, peeled pistachios, walnuts, peeled hazelnuts). Stir over the heat until the sugar syrup caramelizes. Remove from the heat and stir in 50 g (1 2/3 oz) unsalted butter, then pour on an oiled marble surface. As the mixture cools, separate the nuts and transfer to an oiled cooling rack.

Prunes/Raisins

Make a syrup with 1 L (1 qt) water and 1.2 kg (2 1/2 lbs) sugar. Choose moist, high quality dried fruits and pack them loosely in a glass jar. Add 1/5 syrup and 4/5 alcohol of choice*. Cover and place in a cool, dark place to macerate several weeks before using.

For pitted prunes: use Armagnac

For raisins: use rum plus 1 vanilla bean

Decorating with chocolate

Tempering covering chocolate

Covering chocolate, by definition, has a minimum cocoa butter content of 31%.

Due to its high cocoa butter content, covering chocolate is more fluid when melted. When it cools, it hardens with a shiny appearance and creamy texture. Covering chocolate must be used for making the decorations described here.

Covering chocolate is available in dark, white, colored, milk chocolate and flavored.

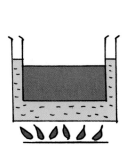 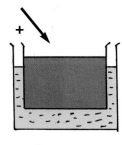 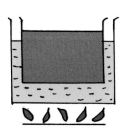

1. Melt 2/3 of the chocolate to 40-50 C (115 F) according to package directions.

2. Off the heat, stir 1/3 of the chocolate (chopped) to cool it to 24-27 C (80 F).

3. Warm the chocolate to 28-32 C (88-90 F), depending on the type of chocolate.

Tempering chocolate over a water bath

Procedure for tempering

1. Melt 2/3 of the chocolate to between 40-50 C (115 F) over a water bath or in the microwave (but not over direct heat). See chart at right for temperatures for various chocolates.

2. Stir in 1/3 of the chocolate (chopped) to cool it to 24-27 C (80 F).

3. Reheat the mixture over a water bath or in a microwave, stirring until it reaches 30-32 C (88-90 F) for bittersweet and 29 C (84-85 F) for milk and white chocolates.

At this point, the chocolate is ready to use.

Type of chocolate	Melt	Cool	Ready to use
Dark	50°	27°	31/32°C
Milk	45°	26°	29/30°C
White	40°	25°	28°C

Advice! Also check the procedure for tempering recommended by the manufacturer.

The principle types of chocolate decorations

A - Made with one type of chocolate   *(shavings, disks)*
B - Made with two types of chocolate   *(bark, marbled disks)*
C - Molded chocolate   *(domes and egg shapes)*
D - Sprayed chocolate coating   *(to finish the top of a dessert)*
E - Made with non-tempered covering chocolate
F - Truffles   *(fans)*

 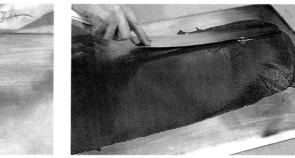 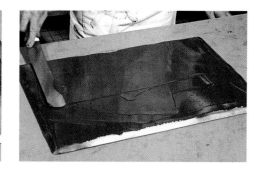

A - Decorations made with one type of chocolate

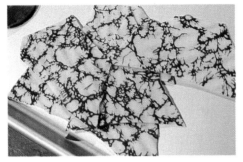

Pressed chocolate pieces (éclats)

Pour a little tempered dark covering chocolate on a sheet of stiff plastic. Place a second sheet on top and press with a rolling pan to make the chocolate as thin as possible.
Chill 1 hour at 15 C (60 F), then break apart and use as needed.

Poured chocolate pieces

Pour a little tempered dark covering chocolate on a sheet of plastic and spread into a thin, even layer.

Chill 1 hour at 15 C (60 F) then break into pieces and use as needed.

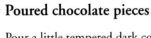

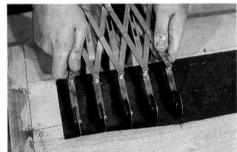

Chocolate strands ("éclaboussures")

Use a whisk with the tips cut off (also used to make spun sugar) and dip the ends in tempered dark covering chocolate. Wave the whisk over a sheet of heavy plastic letting the chocolate fall in strands. Chill for 1 hour at 15 C (60 F), until firm and shiny, then break off what is needed.

Chocolate rectangles

Spread a thin layer of tempered dark covering chocolate on a sheet of stiff plastic. Allow the chocolate to set a few seconds then score rectangles with a multi-bladed cutter (see equipment). Chill 1 hour at 15 C (60 F). Release the chocolate from the plastic sheet and break apart at the straight markings.

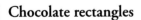

Decorations made with one type of chocolate (continued)

Decorated chocolate pieces

Pour a little tempered dark covering chocolate on a sheet of embossed heavy duty plastic and spread to a thin, even layer. Chill 1 hour at 15 C (60 F), then release the chocolate by twisting the plastic. Break the chocolate into pieces and use as needed.

Chocolate curls/rings ("bouclettes")

Pour a little tempered dark covering chocolate on a sheet of plastic. Use a pastry comb to make a design on the surface, then roll the plastic to join the two sides of chocolate and stick them together. Chill 1 hour at 15 C (60 F), then cut into different sizes.

  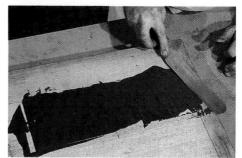

 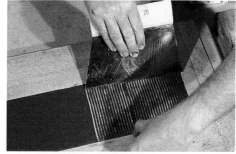  

Chocolate shavings ("copeaux")

Pour tempered dark covering chocolate on a chilled marble working surface and allow to set a few seconds until firm but still pliable, trim the edges. Use a flexible filleting knife or sharp-bladed triangular spatula to scrape the chocolate into shavings.

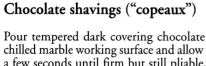   

19

Decorations with one type of chocolate (continued)

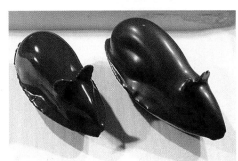

Coating with chocolate

Temper the chocolate in a wide metal bowl.

a/ "Chestnut Mice"

For the chocolate to adhere to the chestnut cream, it is necessary to chill the "mice" in advance in the freezer.
Insert the point of a paring knife securely into

one end of the pastry shell. Use this "handle" to dip the mice and coat them completely without getting chocolate on the pastry. Drain excess chocolate and cool to set. Decorate with royal icing and chocolate glaze piped with a paper cone.

b/ Pineapple "Pavé"

Chill the pavés briefly in the freezer. Take one at a time and hold the top and bottom between your thumb and index finger. Dip each side into the chocolate and place on a sheet of parchment paper to drain. Decorate before serving.

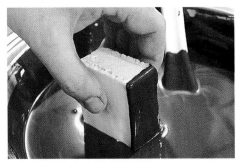

B - Decorations made with two types of chocolate

Bark and twigs ("faux-bois")

Use a rubber roller embossed with a wood grain design. Dip the roller in tempered dark covering chocolate (just like paint), and roll the design on a sheet of sturdy plastic. Cover the band of wood design with a thin coat of tempered white covering chocolate. Place a second sheet of plastic on top and press to make the chocolate very thin and flat. Chill 1 hour at 15 C 960 F). Break apart the "bark" as needed.

Marbled disks

Dip a pastry brush into tempered dark covering chocolate and brush streaks on a sheet of sturdy plastic. Spread a thin layer of white chocolate on top and allow to set a few seconds. Cut circles with round cutters (the sizes needed for decoration). Chill 1 hour at 15 C (60 F), then remove the circles with a spatula.

Striped Triangles

Spread a thin layer of tempered white covering chocolate on a sheet of stiff plastic. Make stripes with a pastry comb while the chocolate is still soft. Allow to set a few seconds then spread a thin layer of dark chocolate on top. Allow to set a few seconds then use a triangular spatula to make triangles in the chocolate. Chill for 1 hour at 15 C (60 F) then remove the triangles from the plastic.

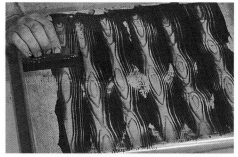
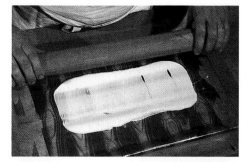

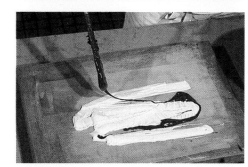

Decorations made with two types of chocolate (continued)

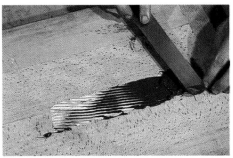

Striped "tear drop"

Cut strips of stiff plastic to fit inside a tear drop-shaped mold. Spread a thin layer of tempered white covernig chocolate then make stripes by scraping with a pastry comb. Allow to set a few seconds before spreading with a thin layer of dark chocolate. Allow to set until firm but still pliable. Bend the plastic strip with the chocolate on the inside and insert into the mold so that the chocolate hardens in the tear drop shape. Chill 1 hour at 15 C (60 F), remove the mold and peel off the plastic.

Two toned cigarettes

Pour tempered white covering chocolate on a chilled marble work surface then spread to a thin, even layer. Scrape with a pastry comb to make stripes. Allow to set a few seconds then pour about the same amount of chocolate to cover the combed band and spread to a thin even layer. Allow to set again a few seconds. Place a sharp triangular metal spatula at a 45 degree angle about 2 inches from the end of the band. Scrape the chocolate away from you with one swift movement to form each cigarette.

C - Molded chocolate

Chocolate dome

Clean the inside of a dome-shaped mold. Temper the chocolate and brush a thin layer on the inside of the dome. Allow to set a few seconds. Pour chocolate to the top then pour off the excess, leaving a thin shell. Trim the rim to make a neat edge and chill 1 hour at 15 C (60 F).

To unmold the dome, press lightly on the inside and twist the chocolate dome and release it onto your hand.

Preparing the chocolate (p. 23)

Mix 50% covering chocolate with 50% cocoa butter. Melt together to 40 C (104 F) then lower the heat to 32 C (89 F). Pour through a very fine strainer to remove any particles then fill the spray gun (a paint sprayer works well).

D - Decorating with Sprayed Chocolate

Keep the sprayer in a warmer at 35 C (95 F) which keeps the chocolate at the perfect temperature for spraying.

Coating a mold

Hold the gun about 50 cm (20 in) from the dome-shaped mold and spray the inside with a sparse coating of chocolate. Allow tro set a few seconds then pour tempered white covering chocolate to the top, pour off excess and chill 1 hour at 15 C (60 F). Unmold th two toned dome.

Coating a dessert

Spray the chocolate from about 50 cm (20 in), moving the gun back and forth to apply an even coating. Tape paper to the wall behind the dessert to catch the spray from around the dessert.

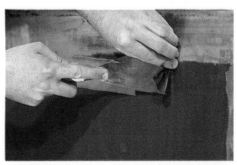

E - Decorating with Non-Tempered Chocolate

Fans ("plissées")

Pour melted covering chocolate (warmed to 50 C (120 F) onto a stainless baking sheet also warmed to 120 F. Spread with an off set spatula to make a thin even layer. Refrigerate for 30 minutes.
Let stand at room temperature until the chocolate becomes slightly pliable. Use a triangular spatula to form fans and pinch the ends to seal.

F - Truffles

Grand Marnier truffles

Make a chocolate ganache flavored with Grand Marnier. Pour into a shallow dish and chill until firm but soft. Pipe out small dollops onto a baking sheet and refrigerate 1 hour. Roll between your hands to make balls. Dip in tempered dark covering chocolate, chill 1 hour, then dust with cocoa powder. Shake in a strainer to remove excess cocoa and keep in a cool, dry place.

Decorations Made with Cooked Sugar

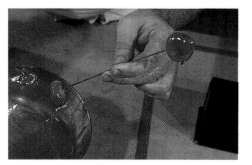

Basic Recipe

350 ml (12 fl oz) water, 1 kg (2.2 lbs) sugar, 200 g (7 oz) glucose

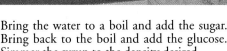

Bring the water to a boil and add the sugar. Bring back to the boil and add the glucose. Simmer the syrup to the density desired.

Precautions to take

When the sugar is dissolving, brush down the sides of the pot with a pastry brush dipped in water to avoid sugar crystals from forming.
Skim away all impurities that rise to the surface with a strainer dipped in cold water.
To stop the cooking process when the correct density is reached, plunge the pot into a bowl filled with cold water for a few seconds. Be careful to not let water drip into the pot.

A. Marronnettes

Mold sweetened chestnut purée to resemble chestnuts. Cook sugar syrup to 130 C (265 F), add red food coloring and heat to 155 C (318 F).Stop the cooking in cold water. Use a long-handled fork or skewer to dip each "marronnette" into the colored sugar syrup. Leave a little hole in the sugar at one end. When the sugar hardens, remove the fork.

Decorations Made with Cooked Sugar (continued)

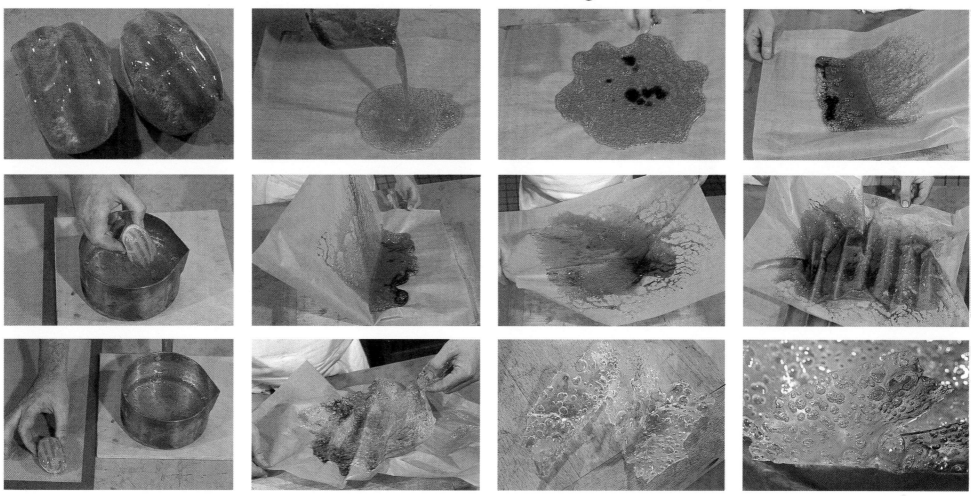

B. Sugar glaze for "salambos"

Cook sugar syrup to (155 C (318 F)) and stop the cooking in cold water. Dip the top of the salambos in the syrup, then invert onto parchment or silicon sheets to harden with a flat top.

C. Poured sugar

Cook sugar syrup to 155 C (318 F) but do not stop the cooking. (Note: In France, special sheets are available for working with hot syrup. A double thickness of parchment held tightly on the ends can be used.) Pour the syrup on the work sheet. Add a few drops of food color and roll the sugar over the sheet, marbling the colors. When the sugar has hardened, break into decorative pieces.

D. Spun sugar

E. Sugar cage

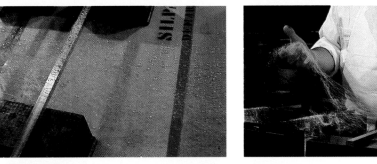   

Place parchment paper or a silicon sheet on the work surface. Prop thin bars or poles of some kind, that have been rubbed with oil, on top of cake pans to catch the spun sugar as it falls. Cook the sugar syrup to 165 C (330 F) and stop the cooking in cold water.

Dip a whisk with tips cut off in the syrup and wave back and forth over the work surface letting the strands of sugar fall from the whisk. When there are enough strands, carefully pick them up and wrap them around the dessert.

Rub oil on the outside of a large ladle. Cook the syrup to a light caramel, 165 C (330 F) and stop the cooking in cold water. Allow the syrup to cool and thicken slightly. Dip a fork in the syrup and drizzle syrup in thin strands over the ladle, crossing back and forth to make a woven

"cage". Leave the sugar to harden on the ladle, then unmold.

Decorating with Sauces and Glazes

A. Decorating with sauces

Basic technique

Ladle a little sauce in the center of the plate and twirl the plate back and forth to cover the plate to the rim.

Decorating part of the plate

Use a small ladle or spoon to place a little sauce to one side in a "free form" pattern.

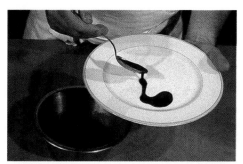

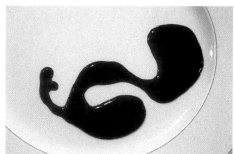

Marbled sauces

Cover part of the plate with sauce (flavored crème anglaise or fruit coulis). Pipe a line with a paper cone with a sauce in a contrasting color (crème fraîche on a coulis, chocolate glaze on a crème anglaise, for example). Swirl the sauces together with the point of a paring knife to create a marbled effect.

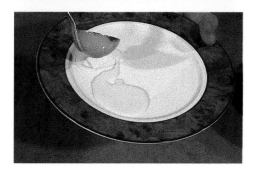

Decorating with Sauces and Glazes (continued)

"Spider web"

Coat the bottom of a plate with sauce (chocolate sauce for example). With a paper cone, pipe a spiral with crème fraîche. Draw the point of a paring knife through the sauces at even intervals, starting in the center straight out to the edge then from the edge to the center.
The design also can be made with a base of crème anglaise with chocolate glaze piped with a paper cone.

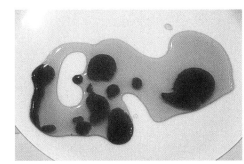

Swirling two sauces

Start with the lighter of the two sauces, caramel sauce for example. Spoon the caramel on the plate in an irregular pattern. Do the same with a dark fruit coulis (for example). Swirl the sauces together with the point of a paring knife.

Oak leaf

Spoon sauce on one side of the plate in a leaf shape. Draw a knife through the sauce around the edge to make the points of an oak leaf.

Adding cocoa powder to sauce

Start with a base of crème anglaise on the plate and place dots of cocoa powder with the point of a knife.

Piping sauce "drops" with a paper cone

With a paper cone, pipe a thin outline of a drop with chocolate glaze.
Spoon sauce in a contrasting color in the center of the "drop".

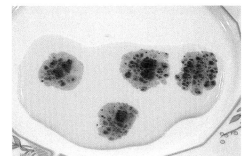

Glazing an unmolded dessert

While a dessert is still in the pastry ring (and well chilled), glaze can be applied in a very smooth layer. Pour a little glaze on top. Hold the mold tightly with one hand and draw a spatula straight across the top, level with the top of the mold to smooth the glaze.

Glazing a dessert on a sheet pan

Use a large off set spatula to spread the glaze evenly over the surface of a large dessert (well chilled) that is still on the baking sheet.

Decorating with glaze piped with a paper cone

(left page, at the bottom)

Fill a paper cone with chocolate or jelly glaze and pipe fancy designs directly on the plate.

Jelly glaze marbled with coffee syrup

Swirl a little coffee syrup into melted apricot jelly glaze and apply it with care to keep the mar-

bled effect. (Note: "extrait de café" is a coffee syrup used often by French pastry chefs to deepen the color and flavor of foods.)

Jelly glaze with cocoa powder

Sprinkle cocoa powder on top of the dessert then carefully apply a light jelly glaze so that the cocoa powder is visible. Smooth the top as described.

Chocolate glaze designs

Spread a thin layer of chocolate glaze on a sheet of stiff plastic. Make stripes (straight or wavy) with a pastry comb) and place in the freezer for 30 minutes to freeze solid.

Place the plastic sheet on a small baking sheet for stability. Place a pastry ring on top of the design and assemble the dessert in reverse (layers of mousse and cake, for example), so that the design will be on top when the dessert is inverted. Chill in the freezer for 1 hour, then flip the dessert onto a plate remove the baking sheet, then peel away the plastic sheet to reveal the design imbedded in the dessert.

Basic recipes for jelly glazes

Light jelly glaze: 400 g (14 oz) strained apricot jam ("nappage blond" is ready made for pastry chefs), 150 g (5 oz) pear syrup, 100 g (3 1/2 oz) glucose
Bring to a boil and strain.

Green jelly glaze: light glaze with green food color

Walnut glaze: Light glaze with chopped walnut nougatine

Red jelly glaze: 400 g (14 oz) red currant jelly ("nappage rouge" is ready made for pastry chefs), 150 g (5 oz) black currant syrup, 100 g (3 1/2 oz) glucose
Bring to a boil and strain.

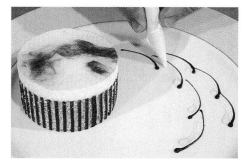

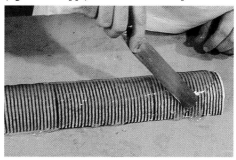

Decorative Cakes, Candies and Cookies

A - Almond sponge cake with a striped design

This technique is very popular in modern dessert making. The method is the same for any design:
1. Make a chocolate cigarette cookie batter (similar to "tuiles").
2. Pipe the desired design on a silicon sheet.
3. Place the sheet in the freezer to firm the batter.

4. Make an almond-flavored sponge cake and spread a thin layer of batter over the frozen design. Bake at 230/240 C (450/475 F) a few minutes.
5. Let the cake cool slightly before removing the silicon sheet.

The following designs can be made using the described method:
Paper cone: Pipe diagonal lines of chocolate batter on the silicon sheet. Place in the freezer.

Striped: Spread a layer of batter and make stripes with a pastry comb.
Place in the freezer.
Streaked: Dip a pastry brush in the batter and apply the batter in streaks across the silicon sheet. Place in the freezer.
Wood grain: Roll the rubber roller with wood grain design in the chocolate batter then roll over the silicon sheet in a wavy, "wood-like" pattern. Place in the freezer.

Chocolate cigarette cookie batter

40 g (1 1/3 oz) powdered sugar, 40 g (1 1/3 oz) egg whites, 40 g (1 1/3 oz) melted butter, 20 g (2/3 oz) flour, 20 g (2/3 oz) cocoa powder
Whisk together the egg whites and the powdered sugar. Blend in the melted butter. Sift the flour and cocoa powder together and stir into the mixture until smooth.

B - Ladyfingers

Make the classic ladyfinger batter. On parchment or silicon sheet, pipe in lines 5 mm (1/4 in) apart with a small plain tip (1 cm (3/8 in)). The lines expand and bake together in a lined sheet of cake.
Bake at 220 C (425 F) until golden and "springy" to the touch.

With sugar: Dust with powdered sugar just before baking.
With cocoa: Dust with cooa powder just before baking.

C - "Croustillants"

(recipe in chapter 6)

100 g (3 1/2 oz) sugar, 70 g (2 1/3 oz) honey, 70 g (2 1/3 oz) butter, 130 ml (6.5 fl oz) heavy cream, 100 g (3 1/2 oz) candied orange peel, chopped, 170 g (6 oz) sliced almonds, 40 g (1 1/3 oz) candied cherries, cchopped, 50 g (1 2/3 oz) flour.

Cook the sugar, honey, butter and cream to 105 C (210 F). Off the heat, stir in the other ingredients.

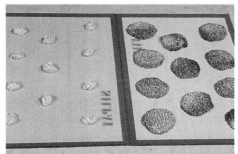

D - Florentines

(recipe in chapter 6)

Spoon florentine batter on silicon sheets and flatten. Bake at 200 C (400 F). Halfwaythrough cooking, when set but not crispy, shape them into perfect circles with a round cutter.

Keep the baked cookies in an air-tight container.

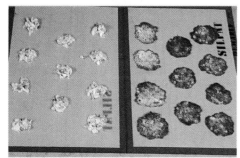

Decorative Cakes, Candies and Cookies (continued)

nougatine. Keep the shapes in an air tight container in a cool place.

Disks: Roll out the nougatine and cut with round cutters.

Rectangles: Roll out the nougatine and cut with a chef's knife.

Triangles: Roll out the nougatine and cut bands 20 cm (8 in) long and 3-4 cm (1 2/ in) wide. Cut into triangles with a chef's knife.

Tart shells: Roll out the nougatine and cut out circles or ovals to fit into individual tart molds. Press the shapes into the oiled molds and remove when hardened.

Chopped nougatine: Use the scraps of nougatine left from making shapes to make a pretty garnish. Hit the pieces with the end of a rolling pin to break into little pieces.

F - Molded cookies

100 g (3 1/2 oz) butter, 100 g (3 1/2 oz) powdered sugar, 100 g (3 1/2 oz) egg whites, 75 g (2 1/2 oz) flour, vanilla extract
(Similar to "tulips" can be molded into shapes, containers.)
Cream the butter and stir in the powdered sugar. Blend in the egg whites (room temperature), then the flour and vanilla. Blend until smooth, let rest 30 minutes.

E - Nougatine

Almond: 300 g (10 oz) fondant, 200 g (7 oz) glucose, 250 g (8 oz) sliced almonds

Walnut: 300 g (10 oz) fondant, 200 g (7 oz) glucose, 250 g (8 oz) chopped walnuts

Melt the glucose and stir in the fondant. Bring slowly to a boil. Add the nuts and continue to cook until the sugar darkens to the desired color. Pour the nougatine onto a silicon sheet.

Shaping nougatine:
To make shaping easier work near a heat source to keep the nougatine pliable (warm oven, sugar lamp). Rub the work surface, rolling pin and cutters with oil to keep the nougatine from sticking.
Warm the nougatine at 170 C (340 F) until soft. Roll out like dough and shape hwile still warm. It may be necessary to tap the top of a cutter with the rolling pin to cut through the

Pipe batter in strips 6 mm (1/4 in) long and cook at 200 C (400 F) until lightly browned. Mold the cookies while still warm.

G - Filo pastry

Melt butter. Cut the filo sheets into whatever shape is needed and brush lightly with butter. Bake on parchment or silicon sheets until golden. If too fragile, brush butter between two sheets and cut a double thickness. Turn to brown on both sides.

Basic Techniques and Tricks of the Trade

A - Filling small tart molds (for the base for the "Chestnut Mice")

Line up the barquette molds side by side on the work surface.

Roll out the pastry to a thin sheet and lay over the molds.

Take a small ball of dough and press the rolled pastry into the molds.

Pass the rolling pin over the top to cut the dough against the rims of the molds.

Trim each mold with a paring knife to make a neat edge.

Pipe almond cream in the bottom and chill.

 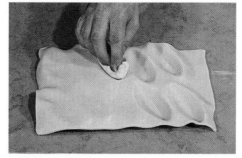 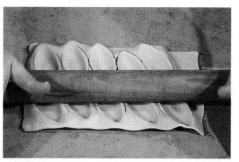

B - Lining an individual mold with cake

Cut a flexible sheet of cardboard to fit the inside of the mold.

Use this template as a guide to cut strips of cake 2/3 the height of the mold and cut to the length that will line the mold all around.

Place the band of cake in the mold. Cut circle of cake to fit in the center.

Brush the cake with syrup and pipe the filling inside.

Chill until firm and unmold.

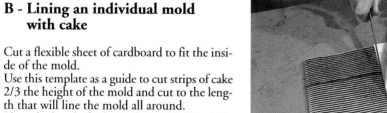   

Basic Techniques and Tricks of the Trade (continued)

C. **Filling a log-shaped mold:**
Line the mold with slices of fruit, or sheets of cake. Chill then fill with mousse or other filling.
Examples here:
Lining the mold with orange slices: orange log cake
Lining the mold with sponge cake: black currant log cake

D. **Assembling the dessert in a rectangular mold: "Blackberry Pavé"**

E. Filling a dome-shaped mold:
Lining the mold with fruit slices:
orange dome
Lining the mold with ice cream:
praline dome

F. Using a pastry bag (plain tip):
"mice"/coffee cream

G. Shaping with a spoon:
"croustillants" with red fruits

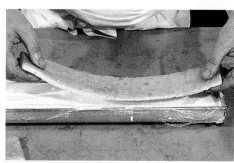

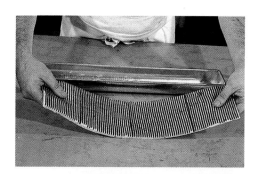

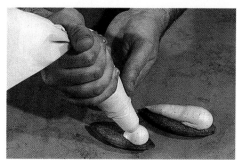

Chapter 2 - Assorted Fresh Fruit Desserts

Introduction
Fresh Summer Fruits

Desserts that call for "fresh fruits" should always be made with the ripest, most flavorful fruits of the season. Apricots and peaches are two of the best fruits of the summer.

1. Fresh Fruit Charlotte
2. Harlequin Tart
3. "Croustillants"
4. Fresh Fruits in Crispy Pastry
5. Warm Apricot Tart
6. Peach and Almond Delight

Fresh Fruit Charlotte

Fresh fruits adorn the top of this elegant vanilla charlotte which is served with a colorful red fruit coulis.

Ingredients

	Decoration
Ladyfingers	Fresh fruits
Vanilla sugar syrup	Jelly glaze
Sponge cake	*Sauce*
Vanilla bavarian cream	Red fruit coulis

Procedure
Cut bands of the ladyfingers 2/3 the height of the small, high-sided pastry rings and long enough to line the molds. Cut circles of sponge cake to fit in the bottom and moisten with vanilla syrup.
Fill the mold with vanilla bavarian, smooth the top, cover and place in freezer about 2 hours or until set.
Prepare the fresh fruits and make the red fruit coulis.

Plate Presentation
When the charlotte is firm, remove the mold and place it on the plate. Arrange the fruits on top, making the most of the shapes and colors of the fruits. Brush with melted jelly glaze and spoon coulis around the charlotte.

Fresh fruits

Vanilla bavarian

Ladyfingers

Sponge cake with vanilla syrup

Harlequin Tart with Fresh Fruits

Use the freshest, most colorful fruits of the season for this tart that combines a sweet pastry crust, light sponge cake and vanilla cream.

Ingredients

Sweet pie pastry
Sponge cake
Vanilla sugar syrup
Vanilla pastry cream
Fresh, seasonal fruits

Decoration
Light jelly glaze

Procedure

Cut circles of pie pastry (3 1/2 in) and press the pastry circles into tart rings (7 cm (3 in)). Prick the bottom with a fork and bake at 200 C (400 F) about 8-10 minutes or until golden and crisp. Remove the molds, place on a rack to cool and trim the edges if necessary. Cut circles from a sheet of sponge cake, moisten with vanilla-flavored sugar syrup.
Make the vanilla pastry cream and prepare the fruits.

Plate Presentation

Place the moistened sponge cake in the bottom of the baked tart crust. Spread a layer of pastry cream on the cake. Place the fruits on top in an attrative pattern. Brush the fruits with melted jelly glaze and place the tart in the center of a small plate.

Fresh fruits with jelly glaze

Vanilla pastry cream

Sponge cake with vanilla syrup

Sweet pie pastry

"Croustillants"

This dessert is a refreshing combination of ripe fruits, a light vanilla cream and crispy cookies ("croustillants") made with orange zest.

Ingredients

Orange croustillants
Vanilla pastry cream
Whipping cream
Fresh fruits, peeled, sliced

Decoration:
Fresh mint leaves for decoration

Sauce:
Caramel sauce with orange

Plate Presentation

Fold the whipped cream into the pastry cream.
(If preparing this dessert to order in a restaurant, make just enough of the lightened cream for each serving.)
Place one cookie on the plate and spoon some vanilla cream on top. Arrange a few slices of fruit on the cream, cover with another cookie. Make a second layer with cream and fruit, top with another cookie.
Pour the orange caramel sauce around the sides, arrange slices of fresh fruit around the cookies and decorate with fresh mint leaves.

Procedure

Whisk together the cookie ingredients and spread very thin circles of the batter on a heavy baking sheet. Bake until browned, transfer to a cooling rack then store in an air tight container.
Make the vanilla pastry cream and cool.
Combine sugar with a little water and cook to a light caramel, add orange juice to dissolve the caramel, simmer to thicken the sauce.
Set aside to cool.
Peel and slice the fruits.
Just before serving, whip the cream to firm peaks.

Fresh Fruits
in Crispy Pastry

The crispy filo dough envelopes with almond cream is a delicious contrast to the fresh fruits.

Ingredients

Filo pastry sheets
Unsalted butter (melted)
Almond cream
Fresh fruits
Currant jelly

Decoration:
Fresh fruits
Fresh mint leaves

Sauce:
Coulis of red fruits

Procedure

For each serving spoon two heaping tablespoons of almond cream onto a square of filo dough.
Arrange fresh, sliced fruits on top and bake at 200 C (400 F) for about 15 minutes.
Make the coulis of mixed red fruits.

Plate Presentation

Just before serving, butter a sheet of filo and place an almond base with fruits in the center and spoon a little currant jelly on top.
Fold the filo dough like an envelope and bake at 200 C (400 F) a few minutes or until golden.
Serve with the fruit coulis and garnish the plate with fresh fruits.
Serve while still warm from the oven.

Warm Apricot Tart

This simple tart is often seen in French pastry shops when apricots from southern France are in season. With good quality canned apricots, the tart can be made anytime and served warm from the oven.

Ingredients

Puff pastry
Egg glaze
Apricot halves in syrup
Sugar

Decoration:
Apricot jam (melted)

Plate Presentation

Serve the freshly baked tart on a warmed plate.

Procedure

Roll out the puff pastry 2 mm (about 1/12 in). Cut out squares 13 cm (5 in), cover with plastic wrap and refrigerate 1 hour.
Place the pastry squares on a heavy baking sheet and brush egg glaze around the edges of each pastry.
Drain the apricots and wipe off excess syrup with paper towels. Arrange several apricot halves in the center of each pastry, leaving a 1/3 inch border around the edge.
Bake at 230 C (450 F) about 20-30 minutes or until the pastry is golden brown.
Sprinkle the baked tarts with sugar and caramelize the sugar under the broiler.
The top can be further embellished with a shiny glaze of apricot jam which has been warmed (to liquify it), strained and brushed over the apricots.

Peach and Almond Delight

This elaborate dessert combines the subtle flavor of peaches with almond and chocolate. The poaching syrup from the peaches can be used to moisten the cake layers. The serving plate is decorated with two contrasting sauces.

Ingredients

Almond sponge cake
(striped with chocolate)
Chocolate sponge cake
Peach mousse
Peaches in syrup

Decoration:
Raspberries
Apricot jam (for glaze)
Cocoa powder

Sauces:
Caramel sauce
Black currant "coulis"

Procedure

Line small pastry rings with strips of the striped sponge cake.
Place slices of chocolate sponge cake in the bottom and brush with peach syrup. Fill each mold with peach mousse with diced peaches added to it.
Firm the mixture in the freezer for about 2 hours.
Make the caramel sauce and the cassis "coulis".
Slice the peaches.
After the desserts have set, dust the top of each mousse with cocoa powder then carefully brush melted and strained apricot (or peach) jam on the top to make them shine.

Plate Presentation

Remove the pastry rings and place each dessert on a large plate. Pour the two sauces on the plate and decorate with raspberries and slices of peaches.

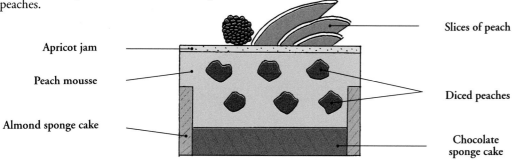

Apricot jam

Peach mousse

Almond sponge cake

Slices of peach

Diced peaches

Chocolate
sponge cake

Introduction   **Red Fruits**

French pastry chefs often combine the colors and flavors of many red fruits for a dazzling display and wonderful taste.
Strawberries, raspberries, black raspberries, red currants, and wild strawberries should be used when in season.

1. "Croustillants" with Red Fruits
2. Raspberry Dome
3. Red Fruit Tart
4. Black Raspberry "Pavé"
5. Napoleon with Strawberries

Raspberry "Croustillants" with Red Fruits

The French often combine several ripe red fruits for a stunning visual effect as well as a delicious blend of sweet and tart flavors. The deep purple black currant "coulis" and crispy raspberry croustillants set off this simple-to-make dessert.

Ingredients

Raspberry croustillants
Whipped cream
Red fruits

Decoration:
Fresh mint leaves

Sauce:
Black currant coulis

Procedure

The cookies can be made in advance and kept fresh in an air tight container.
Clean and trim the fruits and make the coulis
In a chilled bowl, whip the cream to soft peaks. This can be done a few hours in advance of serving, covered and refrigerated. Whisk a little just before serving.

Plate Presentation

Assemble these desserts just before serving.
With a large soup spoon, scoop the whipped cream and place three football-shaped dollops on one side of each plate.

Stand the cookies to the side of the scoops of cream and arrange the fruits around in an attractive pattern.

Spoon black currant sauce on the other side of the plate. Decorate with fresh mint leaves.

45

Raspberry Dome

In the modern French kitchen, a delicate fruit mousse takes many exciting forms, such as this dome. It could be made in a ring mold and sliced if individual dome-shaped molds are not available.

Ingredients

Raspberry mousse
Genoise
Raspberry-flavored sugar syrup
Sweet pie pastry
Red currant jelly glaze

Decoration:
Raspberries

Sauce:
Sabayon with raspberry eau-de-vie

Procedure

Fill the molds with the mousse mixture and press a few raspberries into the center. Cut rounds of genoise to fit the bottom of the molds, brush with sugar syrup flavored with raspberry and cover the mousse with the cake.
Place in the freezer to set for about 2 hours.
Make circles of sweet pie pastry (to fit the bottom of the molds) and bake at 200 C (400 F) about 5 minutes.
Make a sabayon using raspberry "eau-de-vie".

Plate Presentation

Unmold each chilled dome onto a circle of pie pastry and brush the top with melted red currant jelly. (If the surface of the mousse is not firm enough to coat neatly with jelly, place in the freezer again for a few minutes to become thoroughly chilled.) Ladle sabayon on the plate and place the dome in the center. Decorate around the dome with fresh raspberries.

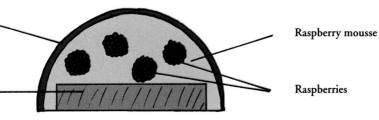

Jelly glaze

Sponge cake with raspberry syrup

Raspberry mousse

Raspberries

Red Fruit Tart

An assortment of red fruits provides a subtle variety of colors as well as flavors. The tartness of the fruits is subdued by the creamy vanilla filling and sauce.

Ingredients

Sweet pie pastry
Genoise
Raspberry-flavored sugar syrup
Vanilla pastry cream
Red jelly glaze

Decoration:
Red fruits

Sauce:
Vanilla crème anglaise

Procedure

Prepare the pie pastry and press circles of dough into 7 cm (3 in) pastry rings. Bake at 200 C (400 F) for 8-10 minutes.
Remove the rings and trim the edge of the baked pastries.
Make the vanilla pasty cream and chill.
Wash, trim and slice (if necessary) the red fruits.
Cut out circles of genoise and brush with sugar syrup.
Make the vanilla crème anglaise and chill.

Plate Presentation

Place the circles of moistened genoise into the base of the pastries.
Cover the cake with a thin layer of pastry cream and arrange the fruits on top in an attractive pattern.
Brush melted red jelly glaze over the fruits to make them shine.
Ladle crème anglaise on the plate and set the tart on top and serve immediately.

Red fruits

Genoise imbibed with
raspberry syrup

Vanilla pastry cream

Sweet pie pastry

47

Black Raspberry "Pavé"

A "pavé (paving stone-shaped cake) is practical for making desserts in large quantities. Slice one portion from the end for restaurant service or divide the whole dessert for a dinner party at home.

Ingredients

Almond sponge cake
Black raspberry-flavored sugar syrup
Black raspberry mousse
Covering chocolate
Red jelly glaze

Decoration:
Raspberry croustillants
Fresh black raspberries
Fresh mint leaves
Sauces:
Caramel sauce
Black raspberry coulis

Procedure

Cut a rectangle from a sheet of almond sponge cake to fit the bottom of a rectangular pastry form. Brush the cake with melted covering chocolate and let it harden. Turn it over and brush with black raspberry sugar syrup . Place the cake in the bottom of the mold. Fill half way up the mold with black raspberry mousse add a slice of almond sponge cake soaked with syrup then add mousse to the top.

Smooth the top, cover and place in the freezer for 2 hours to set. Make the caramel sauce and a black raspberry coulis. Bake the croustillants and keep them fresh in an air tight container.

Plate Presentation

When the mousse is firm, brush on melted jelly glaze and cool to set. Cut the rectangle into servings about 7 cm X 5 cm (3 in X 2 in). Spoon a little of each of the sauces on the serving plate. Garnish with a cookie, a black raspberry and a fresh mint leaf.

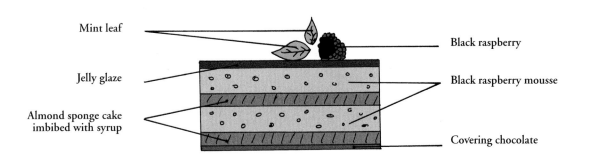

Mint leaf

Jelly glaze

Almond sponge cake imbibed with syrup

Black raspberry

Black raspberry mousse

Covering chocolate

48

Napoleon with Strawberry

This light version of the classic "millefeuille" is made with whipped cream and served with a deep purple sauce of puréed black currants.

Ingredients
Puff pastry (made with butter)
Whipped cream
Raspberry jam

Decoration:
Strawberries
Powdered sugar

Sauce:
Black currant coulis

Procedure

Roll out the puff pastry very thin. Prick the entire surface with a fork or roller docker. Cut rectangles of dough 10 cm X 4 cm (4 in X 1.5 in)). Bake until golden brown, turn the rectangles over and sprinkle powdered sugar on the smooth side. Bake 5 minutes longer to caramelize the sugar. The pastry should be very crispy. Transfer the pastries to a cooling rack.
Make the black currant coulis.
Wash, trim the strawberries, cut in half (if large). Whip the cream.
Assemble each Napoleon with one layer of raspberry jam and one layer of whipped cream between three layers of baked pastry.

Plate Presentation

Using a piping bag with a large tip, pipe four dollops of whipped cream around the edge of the plate. Sprinkle with powdered sugar.
Place strawberries on the mounds of cream and spoon a little more cream on top. Place the Napoleon in the center.
Spoon black currant coulis on the plate.

Strawberries

Whipped cream

Powdered sugar

Raspberry jam

Caramelized puff pastry

Introduction
Black Currants

Black currants or "cassis" are available in France in several forms: fresh, frozen and puréed in jars. So pastry chefs can use this flavorful fruit all year long. The tartness of the berries is best when matched with a sweet fruit such as pears or the subtle taste of almond cream.

1. Almond Tart with Black Currants
2. Black Currant Pyramid
3. Crème Brulée with Black Currants
4. Black Currant Log Cake

Almond Tart with Black Currants

A plain almond tart is made fancy with the addition of black currants. Although blueberries look similar, they are not as firm and would not be a good substitute for the currants in this dessert.

Ingredients

Sweet pie pastry
Fresh black currants
Almond cream
Red jelly glaze

Decorations:
Fresh black currants
Fresh mint leaves

Procedure

Press circles of pie pastry into pastry rings (7 cm (3 in)) and refrigerate 1/2 hour.

Prick the bottom of the pastry with a fork and fill the base with a single layer of fresh black currants. With a spatula or piping bag cover the berries to the rim of the pastry with almond cream.

Bake in a preheated 200 C (400 F) oven 15-20 minutes.

Transfer to a cooling rack.

Plate Presentation

Trim any ragged edges of the cooked pastry with a paring knife or vegetable peeler.

Arrange a single layer of black currants on the top and brush on melted red jelly glaze to make them shine.

Place the tart in the center of the the plate and decorate with a fresh mint leaf.

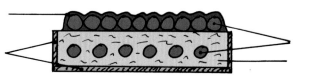

Jelly glaze

Sweet pie pastry

Fresh black currants

Almond creams

Black Currant Pyramid

Pears, puréed to make a sauce for this dessert, marry well with the tart flavor of the black currant mousse. The dessert can be assembled in individual molds of any shape.

Ingredients

Black currant mousse
Genoise
Black currant-flavored sugar
 syrup
Red currant jelly

Sauce:
Pear coulis

Decoration:
Marbled chocolate disks
Poached pears
Coffee syrup
Fresh black currants
Fresh mint leaves

Procedure

Place the individual molds on a sheet of plastic wrap.
Fill with black currant mousse and cover the base with cake moistened with syrup. Place in the freezer for 2 hours to set.
Make the marbled chocolate disks.
Poach the pears. Cut a few slices for each plate and purée the remaining pears with poaching syrup to make a "coulis".

Plate Presentation

Unmold the pyramid of mousse onto a disk of chocolate in the center of a plate. Brush the surface with cool, liquid jelly glaze. (After unmolding, if the the surface of the mousse is too soft to brush on the glaze, return the dessert to the freezer a few minutes.)
Use a squeeze bottle to form a ring of pear sauce around the dessert and garnish the plate with slices of pears. Brush the pears with a little coffee syrup to make them golden and shiny.
Decorate the top of the pyramid with fresh black currants and fresh mint leaves.

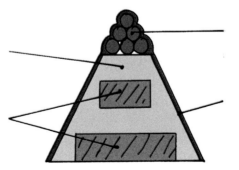

Black currant mousse

Sponge cake moistened
with black currant syrup

Fresh black currants

Red currant glaze

Crème Brulée
with Black Currants

Rich crème brulée custard is improved with a layer of tart and juicy black currants. The brown sugar in France, used to caramelize the top, is the granular type. If you can't fine "sucre roux" (often sold as a fancy sugar to sweeten coffee), white sugar will work better than the moist brown sugar sold for baking.

Ingredients

Crème brulée custard
Fresh black currants
"Sucre roux"

Procedure

Cover the base of the crème brulée molds with a single layer of black currants.
Spoon the custard over the berries and cook at 120 C (250 F) about 25 minutes or until set but still creamy.
Chill the cooked desserts in the refrigerator for several hours.

Plate Presention

Just before serving, sprinkle the top of the crème brulée with sugar.
Caramelize the sugar under the broiler or with a torch.
Place on a plate and serve at once.

Black Currant Log Cake

Hidden beneath the snowy white meringue of this traditional log-shaped cake ("bûche) is a black currant mousse with fresh berries and spongecake imbibed with "cassis"-flavored syrup.

Ingredients

Black currant mousse
Fresh black currants
Genoise
Black currant-flavored sugar
  syrup
Italian meringue

Decoration:
Two-toned cigarette cookies

Sauce:
Black currant "coulis"

Procedure

Line a log shaped mold with plastic wrap then a sheet of genoise. Brush with black currant sugar syrup to moisten and add flavor.

Fill the mold to the top with black currant mousse, adding fresh black currants into the mixture. Cut a rectangle of cake the size of the base, brush with syrup and invert onto the mousse. Place the "bûche" in the freezer for 2 hours to set the mousse. Unmold onto a platter and pipe Italian meringue over the log. Brown the meringue under the broiler or with a torch.

With a knife dipped in hot water, cut a thin slice off each end to give a neat appearance.

Plate Presentation

Cut 2 one inch slices of the mousse per serving and arrange them on the plate. To make neat slices, use a long thin knife dipped in hot water (and wiped clean between slices) to slice the delicate mousse. Spoon black currant sauce around the mousse and decorate with fresh black currants and a cookie.

Italian meringue

Fresh black currants

Genoise with syrup

Black currant mousse

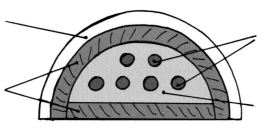

Introduction
Oranges

A century ago, receiving an orange at Christmas was a special treat for children, now they are enjoyed year round. The pastry chef can add the wonderful flavor to desserts in the form of fresh, juicy sections, poached slices or candied peel. Orange is especially good when paired with chocolate, a match made in heaven.

1. Orange Cream with Chocolate
2. Orange Dome
3. Chocolate "Pavé" with Orange
4. Orange Log Cake

Orange Cream with Chocolate

The winning combination of orange and chocolate is featured in this dessert of orange-flavored pastry cream, sections of fresh orange, a caramel orange sauce and bittersweet chocolate

Ingredients

Chocolate disks
Pastry cream, flavored with orange
Whipped cream
Orange sections

Decorations:
Chocolate shavings

Sauce:
Orange caramel sauce

Plate Presentation

Using two soup spoons, form three "football-shaped" dollops ("quenelles") of cream on one side of the plate.
Lean a chocolate disk on each dollop of cream.
Ladle orange caramel sauce on the other side of the plate.
Decorate with 5 segments of orange and chocolate shavings.

Procedure

Make the chocolate disks and keep in a cool, dry place.
Make the light orange pastry cream and orange caramel sauce.
Keep the cream refrigerated until the dessert is assembled.
Cut away the peels of the oranges and remove the sections by cutting between the pith with a small knife.

56

Orange Dome

The translucent slices of orange that cover this dome hint at the flavor of the bavarian inside which features a dice of candied orange peel. The chocolate sauce is the perfect compliment.

Ingredients

Thin slices orange, candied
Orange bavarian
Candied orange peel
Genoise
Orange-flavored syrup
(from poaching the oranges)

Decoration:
Clear jelly glaze or apricot jam

Sauce:
Chocolate sauce
Crème fraîche (for design)

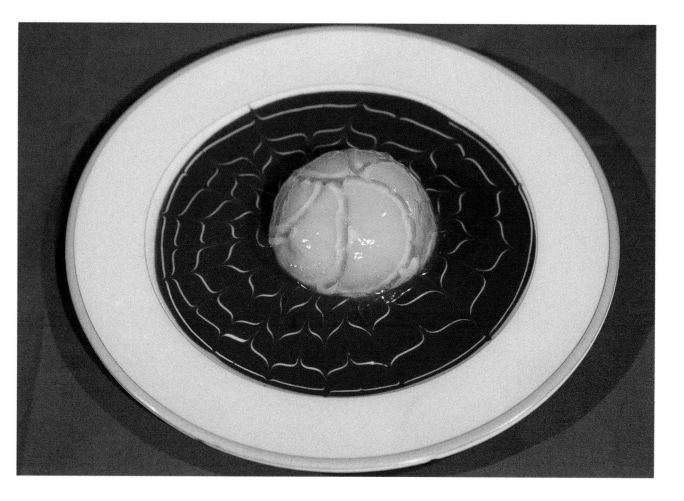

Procedure

Blanch the orange slices then poach in light syrup until translucent.
Line the dome-shaped molds with the slices and place in the freezer for 1/2 hour.
Make the orange bavarian and stir in candied orange peel.
Fill each mold with bavarian cream and cover the top with a circle of genoise moistened with the orange-flavored poaching syrup.
Cover and place in the freezer for 2 hours to set.
Make the chocolate sauce.

Plate Presentation

Unmold the dome and brush on jelly glaze or melted and strained apricot jam to make it shine. Cover the bottom of the plate with chocolate sauce and make a web design with crème fraîche piped with a paper cone. Place the dome in the center of the plate.

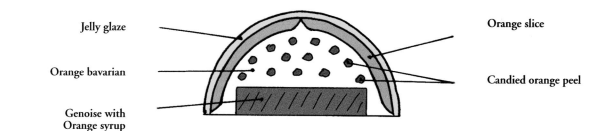

Chocolate "Pavé" with Orange

In French, "pavé" means "paving stone". In restaurants and pastry shops, cakes assembled in a rectangular shape are easily and neatly portioned into individual "pavés".

Ingredients

Orange ganache
Orange pastry cream
Covering chocolate
Orange-flavored sponge cake
Sugar syrup with Cointreau
Apricot jam (for glaze)
Cocoa powder

Decorations:
Fresh orange segments
Chocolate curls

Sauces:
Chocolate sauce
Orange caramel sauce

Ingredients

Make 2 sheets (40 cm X 60 (16 in X 24 in)) of orange-flavored sponge cake. Cut the cooled cakes in half.
With a spatula, cover one strip of cake with melted covering chocolate, cool to set. Turn over and brush all the cake strips with sugar syrup flavored with Cointreau.
With the layer of covering chocolate on the bottom, apply a thin layer of ganache.
Add a layer of cake and cover with orange cream.
Add a layer of cake and cover with ganache.
Finish with the last strip of cake and cover with a thin layer of orange cream. Smooth the top with a knife dipped in hot water. Place in the freezer for 2 hours to set.
Make the chocolate sauce and the orange-flavored caramel sauce.

Plate Presentation

With a sharp knife dipped in hot water, cut the large "pavé" into individual servings (7 cm X 4 cm (3 in X 1 1/2 in)).
Sprinkle the top with cocoa powder then carefully brush on the melted and strained apricot jam (or clear jelly glaze).
Place the small "pavé" on one side of the plate and spoon the two sauces on the other side.
Decorate the top of the dessert with two chocolate curls and two fresh orange segments (or mandarin orange segments brushed with apricot glaze)

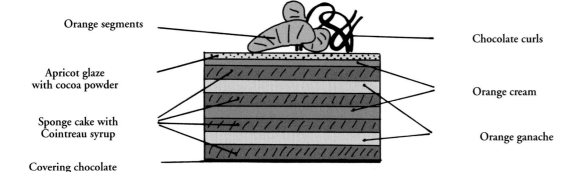

Orange segments

Apricot glaze with cocoa powder

Sponge cake with Cointreau syrup

Covering chocolate

Chocolate curls

Orange cream

Orange ganache

Orange Log Cake

Orange and chocolate make a grand finale to a Christmas dinner in this light version of the traditional "bûche" or yule log cake.

Ingredients

Orange bavarian
Candied orange peel
Chocolate sponge cake
Orange sponge cake
Sugar syrup with Grand Marnier

Decoration:
Chocolate "twigs"
Thin slices of orange, candied
Apricot jam (for glaze)
Sauce:
Orange caramel sauce

Procedure

Line the log-shaped mold with plastic wrap and line the mold with the orange slices (blanched then poached in light syrup). Place in the freezer for 1/2 hour.
Fill the mold with orange bavarian, adding the chopped candied orange peel as you fill the mold.
Cut rectangles of chocolate and orange sponge cake to fit the bottom of the mold, brush with Grand Marnier syrup and place them on top of the cream.
Cover and place in the freezer for 2 hours to set.
Make the orange caramel sauce.
Unmold the firm "bûche", remove the plastic. Return to the freezer to firm the surface then brush with apricot glaze (melted and strained).
Trim the ends with a sharp knife dipped in hot water.
Decorate the sides with chocolate "twigs" (if serving whole).

Plate Presentation

Cut two 1 inch slices of bûche per serving with a sharp knife dipped in hot water. Wipe clean each time a slice is made.
Place the slices on the plate and spoon orange caramel sauce around.
Decorate with chocolate twigs and serve at once.

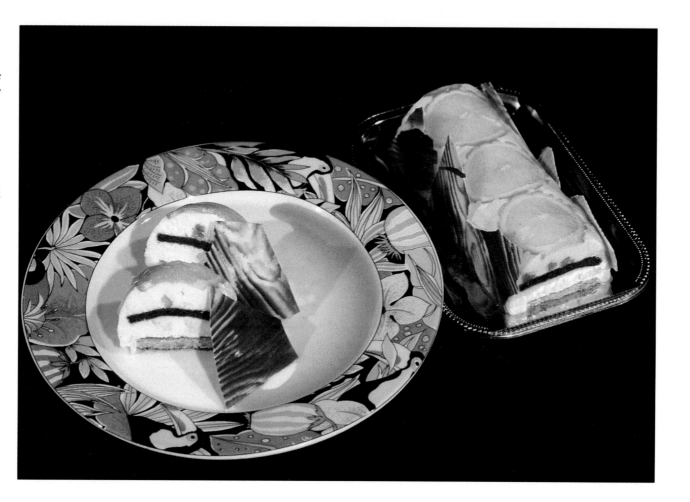

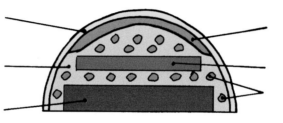

Apricot glaze

Orange slices, candied

Orange bavarian

Chocolate sponge cake
with Grand Marnier syrup

Orange sponge cake
with Grand Marnier syrup

Candied orange peel

59

Introduction   **Lemons**

Lemons give desserts a refreshing taste but the acidity must be balanced carefully with a sweet counterpart. The sauces made with caramel and raspberries presented here work well as does the classic combination of meringue with tart lemon pie filling.

1. Lemon Tart
2. Lemon "Pavé" with Raspberry Coulis
3. Lemon Mousse with Tea-Infused Caramel

Lemon Tart

This classic French "patisserie" favorite is augmented with a garnish of candied lemon peel and currants.

Ingredients

Sweet pie pastry
Lemon curd
Jelly glaze

Decoration:
Julienned candied lemon peel
Thin slices lemon, candied
Currants
Mint leaves

Procedure

Line the pastry rings (7 cm (3 in)) with sweet pie pastry.
Prick with a fork and bake at 200 C (400 F) for 8-10 minutes.
Make the candied lemon peel and lemon slices.
Cook the lemon curd and set aside to cool.
Fill the baked tart shells to the top with the cream and refrigerate for 20 minutes to set the cream.

Plate Presentation

Brush jelly glaze over the cooled tarts.
Decorate the top with 1/2 slice of lemon, a small bunch of currants and a mint leaf.
Serve the candied lemon peel on the side of the tart or pass separately.

Fruit decoration

Jelly glaze

Sweet pie pastry

Lemon curd

Lemon Pavé with Raspberry Coulis

Lemon and raspberry are natural partners in this refreshing dessert. The syrup from cooking the candied lemon peel can be diluted to make a light syrup to moisten the cake layers.

Ingredients

Genoise	Lemon-flavored sugar syrup
Lemon mousseline	Covering chocolate

Procedure

Make a sheet of genoise (40 cm X 60 cm (16 in X 24 in)).
Cut the cooled cake in half.
Coat one strip of cake with melted covering chocolate, cool to set, turn it over and brush the other side with sugar syrup flavored with lemon. Moisten the other strip of cake as well. Cover the first strip of cake with lemon mousse, place a layer of cake on top and finish with a thin, smooth layer of mousse on top.
Place in the freezer about 1 hour to firm the cream.
Make the raspberry sauce, poach the lemon slices in light syrup and candy the lemon peel (slices are more lightly "candied").

Plate Presentation

Sprinkle cocoa powder over the top of the chilled pavé and carefully brush jelly glaze on the top. Cut the chilled dessert into small "pavés" 7 cm X 4 cm (3 in X 1.5 in).
Place the pavé on one side of the plate and spoon raspberry coulis on the other. A design can be made in the sauce by piping a thread of crème fraîche and drawing through the line with the point of a knife.
Garnish the dessert with fresh red currants (or raspberries), julienned candied lemon peel and lemon slices.

Decoration:
Strawberries
Red currants
Mint leaves
Candied lemon peel
Candied lemon slices
Cocoa powder
Jelly glaze

Sauce:
Raspberry coulis
Crème fraîche

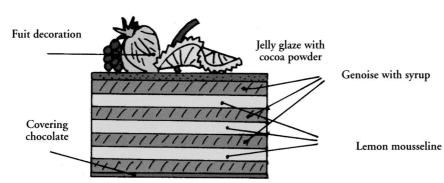

Fuit decoration

Jelly glaze with cocoa powder

Genoise with syrup

Lemon mousseline

Covering chocolate

Lemon Mousse with Tea-infused Caramel

If teardrop-shaped molds are not available, assemble the lemon mousse in any individual mold that is approximately the same depth. The syrup used for cooking the lemon peel can be diluted to moisten the cake layers.

Ingredients

Lemon mousse
Genoise
Lemon-flavored sugar syrup
Nougatine, chopped
Chocolate ganache
Jelly glaze

Decoration:
Nougatine circles
Chocolate shavings
Candied lemon peel
Sauce:
Caramel sauce with tea

Procedure

This dessert is assembled upside down and turned over to unmold. For the decorative top, spread a very thin layer of ganache on a sheet of parchment and make the design with a pastry "comb". Place the molds on the ganache and place in the freezer 15 minutes.

Add lemon mousse to fill the molds 2/3 and sprinkle chopped nougatine (almond brittle) over the mousse.

Cut pieces of spongecake to fit the mold, brush with syrup and invert on top of the mousse. Place in freezer for about 2 hours until set.

Make the nougatine (circles and chopped) and chocolate shavings. To make the sauce, cook sugar to a light caramel and add tea to dissolve the caramel.

Julienne the lemon peel, blanch, then cook in syrup until candied.

Plate Presentation

When the desserts are firm, turn them over, and with one swift move, remove the paper (the mousse must be very firm for the ganache to remain in place).

Brush jelly glaze on the top and remove the mold.

Place the "teardrop" on the disk of nougatine and place on the plate.

Press the chocolate shavings around the side.

Pour the caramel sauce around the dessert and decorate with candied lemon peel.

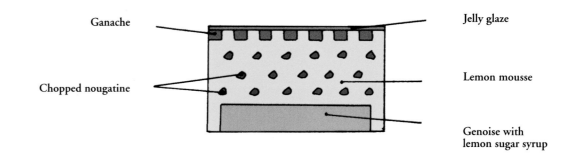

Ganache

Jelly glaze

Chopped nougatine

Lemon mousse

Genoise with lemon sugar syrup

Chapter 3
Desserts Made with Autumn Fruits and Tropical Fruits

Introduction
Apples

Although there are hundreds of apple varieties, it is important to choose an apple that will hold up during cooking. Granny Smith, Red and Golden Delicious, Reinettes and Galas are good cooking apples that are available year round.

1. Granny Smith Mousse with Blackberry Coulis

2. Apple Tart with Calvados Sabayon

3. Granny Smith Sorbet with Sugar Leaves

4. Apple "Millefeuille" with Raspberry Caramel Sauce

5. Apple Brochettes Flamed with Calvados

6. Apple Log Cake

Granny Smith Apple Mousse with Blackberry

Thin slices of apple, flamed with Calvados decorate the top of this delicate apple mousse served with a brilliant sauce of black raspberies. Apple jelly glaze adds flavor and a golden shine.

Ingredients

Apple slices
Granny Smith apple mousse
Genoise
Sugar syrup with Calvados
Sweet pie pastry
Apple jelly glaze

Garnish:
Chocolate shavings
Blackberries

Sauce:
Blackberry coulis

Procedure

Cook the apple slices in the oven with a little butter and sugar and flame with Calvados. Line the pastry rings with plastic wrap and arrange three cooked apple slices in the bottom.
Fill the molds about 3/4 with apple mousse.
Place a round of genoise, moistened with sugar syrup on the mousse then place a circle of baked sweet pie pastry on top.
Cover and place in freezer for about 2 hours to set.
Make the chocolate shavings and blackerry sauce.

Plate Presentation

When the mousse is firm, turn the rings over and remove the molds and plastic wrap. Brush the apples on top with melted apple jelly. Place the mousse on one side of the plate and press chocolate shavings around the sides. Pour blackberry coulis on the other side of the plate and decorate with fresh blackberries.

Apple jelly glaze

Apple mousse

Genoise

Cooked apple slices

Sweet pie pastry

Apple Tart
with Calvados Sabayon

Puff pastry trimmings, left from shaping "millefeuilles" and "feuilletées" are used here because, although the layered dough adds lightness to the tart, the pastry does not need to rise like it does when it "stands alone".

Ingredients

Puff pastry trimmings
Apple slices
Vanilla "chibouste" cream

Sauce:
Sabayon with Calvados

Procedure

Line the pastry rings (7 cm (3 in)) with puff pastry and refrigerate 2 hours. Prick the dough with a fork, line with parchment paper and pie weights (to keep the pastry from puffing too much).
Bake at 200 C (400 F)) for 20-25 minutes.
Remove the weights and paper and return to the oven 5 minutes.
Cook the apples in the oven with a little butter and sugar, flame with Calvados.
Make the "chibouste" and sabayon.

Plate Presentation

Arrange a single layer of cooked apple slices in the bottom of the baked tart shells.
Pipe chibouste on top using a plain 12 mm (1/2 in) tip.
Sprinkle the top with granulated sugar and caramelize the sugar under the broiler or with a torch.
Ladle sabayon on the plate and place the tart in the center

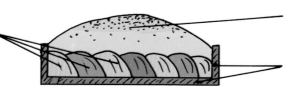

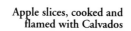

Chiboust cream with
caramelized sugar glaze

Apple slices, cooked and
flamed with Calvados

Puff pastry

Granny Smith Sorbet with Sugar Leaves

The cinnamon in the custard sauce enhances the flavor of the apples and the disks of sugar makes this elegant French dessert as tasty as an old fashioned candy apple.

Ingredients

Granny Smith apple sorbet
Leaves made from cooked sugar
Apple slices
Calvados

Decoration:
Fresh mint leaves
Cinammon sticks

Sauce:
Crème anglaise with cinnamon

Procedure

Cook sugar to the hard ball stage, add green food coloring and pour onto a lightly greased tray to cool. Cut leaf shapes about 5 cm (2 in).
Make the apple sorbet and the cinnamon crème anglaise.
Cook the apple slices in the oven with a little butter and sugar then flame with Calvados.

Plate Presentation

Arrange three scoops of sorbet on one side of the plate and prop the sugar leaves between the scoops. (These "football-shaped" "scoops-quenelles" are shaped with soup spoons, dipped in hot water.)
Spoon the sauce on the plate and add the cooked apple slices. Decorate with a mint leaf and a cinnamon stick.

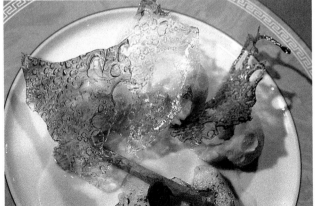

Apple Millefeuille with Raspberry Caramel Sauce

Apples slices, baked in the oven with honey are paired with vanilla cream and crispy pastry all surrounded by a rich raspberry caramel sauce and topped with spun sugar.

Ingredients

Puff pastry
Vanilla pastry cream
Apple slices cooked in honey

Sauce:
Raspberry caramel sauce

Decoration:
Raspberries
Mint leaves
Spun sugar (with red color)

Procedure

Roll out the puff pastry very thin (1 mm (1/20 in)). Prick the entire surface with a roller docker or fork. Cut into rectangles (10 cm X 4 cm (4 in X 1 1/2 in)). Chill the dough for 1 hour then bake at 200 C (400 F) about 20 minutes or until golden brown. Turn over the baked pastries and sprinkle liberally with powdered sugar. Return to the oven to caramelize the sugar. The pastry should be thoroughly baked. Spread vanilla pastry cream on the first rectangle, top with pastry.
Arrange cooked apple slices in the center then top with a third sheet of baked pastry.
Make the raspberry caramel sauce and spun sugar.

Plate Presentation

Place the millefeuille on one side of the plate and set a piece of spun sugar on top. Ladle caramel sauce on the plate and garnish with fresh raspberries and mint leaves.

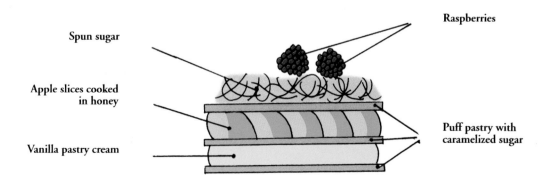

Spun sugar

Apple slices cooked in honey

Vanilla pastry cream

Raspberries

Puff pastry with caramelized sugar

69

Apple Brochette Flamed with Calvados

Warm desserts with apples are wonderful on cold fall days. These brochettes are easy to make.

Ingredients

Apples
Creamy gratin mixture
Calvados

Procedure

Peel and core apples and cut in large dice.
Sprinkle with sugar and melted butter and bake in a hot oven until softened.
Put 6-7 apple pieces on each skewer.
Make the creamy gratin mixture by folding whipped cream into bombe mixture.

Plate Presentation

Spoon gratin mixture into a shallow, heatproof dish.
Place an apple brochette on top.
Brown the top with a salamander or under the broiler.
Just before serving, flame the dessert with Calvados.

Apple Log Cake

Another variation on the traditional Christmas log cake ("bûche"). This delicate mousse, with its creamy, cinnamon sauce can be served year round. The wood grain design on the cake is achieved with a special stencil.

Ingredients

Almond sponge cake
(with wood grain design)
Granny Smith mousse
Apple slices, baked with sugar
Sugar syrup with Calvados
Apple jelly glaze

Decoration:
Cinnamon sticks
Tiny apples
Chocolate disks
Sauce:
Cinnamon créme anglaise

Procedure

Line a bûche mold with plastic wrap then lay a sheet of sponge cake with a wood grain design in the bottom, brush with syrup. Fill with apple mousse, adding cooked apple slices into the mousse. Cut a rectangle of plain sponge cake to fit the bottom, moisten with syrup and invert on top of the mousse.
Cover and place in freezer for about 2 hours to set the mousse.
Unmold, remove the plastic and brush with melted jelly glaze.
For a neat presentation, cut thin slices off the ends.
Make the cinnamon crème anglaise

Plate Presentation

Cut two 1 inch slices of bûche for each serving and arrange on the plate. To cut each slice cleanly, wipe off the knife and dip in hot water each time you slice.
Pour crème anglaise around the dessert and garnish with a tiny apple, a cinnamon stick and chocolate disks.

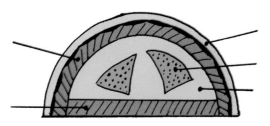

Almond sponge cake
with wood grain design

Jelly glaze

Slices of cooked apple

Apple mousse

Almond spongecake
with Calvados syrup

Introduction
Pears

Pears, which originated in the Middle East, have a subtle flavor that marries well with chocolate and almonds. Certain spices, such as ginger, are also delicious with pears.

1. Pear Mousse

2. Pear Tart

3. Pear Tart with Chocolate

4. Pear Dome

5. Pear Gratin with Ginger

Pear Mousse

The light syrup used to poach the pears can be used to imbibe the cake layers. Chocolate cake and black currant sauce make a dramatic contrast to the delicate mousse. If tiny pears are in season, they can be used for a decoration instead of sliced pears.

Ingredients

Almond sponge cake
Chocolate sponge cake
Pear mousse
Poached pears, diced
Pear-flavored sugar syrup
Cocoa powder
Apple jelly glaze

Decoration:
Chocolate fans
Poached pears, sliced
Coffee syrup

Sauce:
Black currant coulis

Procedure

Cut strips of the almond sponge cake that will line the individual molds about 2/3 the way up the sides.
Cut a circle of chocolate sponge cake and place in the bottom.
Brush syrup on the cake to moisten.
Fill the lined molds with pear mousse and add some diced poached pears in the center.
Cover and place in the freezer for about 2 hours to set. Make the chocolate fans, the black currant coulis and slice the pears.

Plate Presentation

Sprinkle the top of the frozen mousse with cocoa powder and carefully brush on melted apple jelly glaze to make it shine.
Remove the ring and place on the serving plate.
Pour sauce around the mousse. Brush a little coffee syrup on the pear slices (or miniature pears) to make it golden.
Garnish the plate with pears and a chocolate fan.

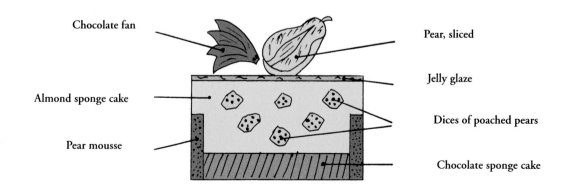

Chocolate fan

Pear, sliced

Almond sponge cake

Jelly glaze

Pear mousse

Dices of poached pears

Chocolate sponge cake

Pear Tart

This classic combination of pears and almond cream is improved with a light puff pastry crust and by flaming the warm tart with pear eau-de-vie just before serving. Pastry trimmings, from making feuilletés, can be used because the pastry does not need to rise.

Ingredients

Puff pastry	Poached pears
Almond cream	Pear eau-de-vie

Procedure

Roll the pastry very thin (2 mm (1/16 in)) and line 12 cm (5 in) pastry rings.
Refrigerate 1 hour.
Prick the bottom with a fork.
With a pastry bag and large plain tip, pipe a layer of almond cream on the bottom of each pastry.
Slice the pears (poached in light syrup) and overlap the slices in a petaled pattern on top of the almond cream.

Plate Presentation

Bake in a preheated oven (220 C (425 F)) for 15 minutes.

Place the freshly baked tart on a heated serving plate and flame at the table with pear eau-de-vie.

Pear Tart with Chocolate

This rich tart combines a thick layer of ganache in a buttery hazelnut crust with pears and a coffee custard sauce. The pears can be poached or baked in the oven with butter and sugar.

Ingredients

Sablée pastry with hazelnuts
Poached pears
Ganache filling for tarts

Decoration:
Chocolate curls
Grand Marnier truffles

Sauce:
Coffee crème anglaise

Procedure

Line 7 cm (3 in) tart rings with hazelnut sablée pastry.
Prick the dough with a fork and bake 200 C (400 F) for 8-10 minutes.
Remove the rings, cool and trim the baked pastries.
Fill the pastries half full with diced poached pears then pour the ganache over the pears. Refrigerate 2 hours to set the ganache.
Make the truffles and the chocolate curls.

Plate Presentation

Transfer the tart to a serving plate.
Ladle the sauce around the tart.
Garnish with chocolate curls and a Grand Marnier truffle.

Truffle

Chocolate curls

Ganache

Poached pears

Hazelnut pastry

Pear Dome

A refreshing combination of poached pear slices and vanilla bavarian molded in a dome-shaped mold then decorated with chocolate. Use the poaching syrup from the pears to imbibe the genoise.

Ingredients

Poached pears
Vanilla bavarian cream
Genoise
Pear-flavored syrup

Decoration:
Chocolate shavings
Apple jelly glaze
Coffee syrup
Sauce:
Chocolate glaze

Procedure

Poach the pears in light syrup, slice very thinly.
Line the dome-shaped mold with pear slices and place in the freezer to keep them in place.
Fill the mold with vanilla bavarian, and cover with a circle of genoise that has been moistened with the pear poaching syrup.
Place in the freezer about 2 hours to become firm.
Make the chocolate glaze and chocolate shavings.

Plate Presentation

Unmold the chilled dome.
Brush a little coffee syrup on the pears to make them golden then brush with jelly glaze to make them shine.
Place the dome in the center of the serving plate.
Decorate with the chocolate shavings and pipe out "drops" with the chocolate glaze.

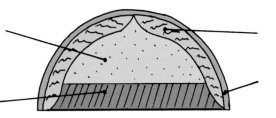

Vanilla bavarian cream

Poached pear slices

Jelly glaze

Genoise moistened
with pear syrup

Pear Gratin
with Ginger

The pears for this warm dessert are poached with ginger, pepper, and clove. Just before serving, they are covered with an egg-based mixture which browns under the broiler.

Ingredients

Poached pears
Creamy gratin mixture

Procedure

Peel 4 pears and remove the seeds and cut each pear into 12 slices.
Prepare a syrup with 500 g (1 lb) sugar, 200 ml (scant 1/2 cup) water, 10 g (3 1/2 oz) chopped fresh ginger, 1 clove, 1 "grind" of freshly ground pepper.
Add the pear slices to the cool syrup, bring to a simmer.
Poach 2-3 minutes and cool in the syrup.
Make the gratin sauce.

Plate Presentation

Remove the pears slices with a slotted spoon and overlap them in a
circle on a heat proof plate.
Ladle the sauce over the pears and brown the top with a salamander or place briefly under the broiler.
Serve hot.

Introduction **Pineapples, Cherries and Grapes**

Choose pineapples that are ripe and juicy for the best results. For some recipes, high quality canned pineapple can be used.

For desserts with cherries, French pastry chefs prefer the flavorful "Amarenas" which are available preserved in syrup. These are especially good in Black Forest Cake. Grapes are rarely used in pastries because for the best results they should be peeled and seeded. Locally grown grapes, sold during the fall season, are delicious in desserts flavored with sweet wines.

1. Black Forest Cake

2. Cherry Bavarian Cream

3. Pineapple Meringue Tart

4. "Africa"

5. Chocolate Triangles with Cherries

6. "Babas" with Grapes and Muscat Sabayon.

7. Chocolate Leaves with Grapes

8. Pineapple "Pavé" with Mango Coulis

Black Forest Cake

This French version of the classic Black Forest cake is beautiful and delicious. The three layers of chocolate sponge cake, moistened with Kirsch, hold a filling of delicate whipped cream and cooked cherries.

Ingredients

Chocolate sponge cake
Sugar syrup with Kirsch
Whipped cream
Cherries

Decoration:
Chocolate shavings

Sauces:
Vanilla crème anglaise
Chocolate glaze

Procedure

Use cooked cherries in syrup.

Assemble the dessert in a tall pastry ring (5 cm (2 in)).

The bottom layer is a circle of chocolate sponge cake, coated with melted covering chocolate on the bottom and moistened with syrup on top. Cover the cake with a 1 cm (3/8 in) layer of whipped cream with cherries on top. Press another moistened cake layer on top, add more cream and cherries and finish with a third circle of sponge cake.

Add whipped cream to the top of the mold and smooth with a metal spatula. Refrigerate 1/2 hour.

Remove the ring and cover the sides with a smooth layer of whipped cream.

Decorate with the chocolate shavings.

Plate Presentation

Place a slice of the cake on the plate.

Ladle crème anglaise on the plate and pipe out a line of chocolate glaze with a paper cone. With the tip of a knife, swirl the sauces to make a web design.

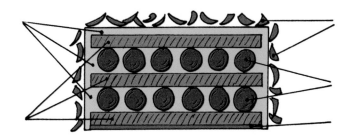

Whipped cream

Chocolate shavings

Cherries

Chocolate sponge cake with Kirsch syrup

Covering chocolate

Cherry Bavarian Cream

Better than a chocolate covered cherry, this dessert combines these two natural flavor partners.

Ingredients

Chocolate sponge cake
Marascino-flavored sugar syrup
Marascino bavarian cream
Cooked cherries

Decoration:
Chocolate disks
White chocolate fans
Cooked cherries
Red jelly glaze
Sauce:
Cherry coulis

Procedure
Place a layer of chocolate sponge cake, moistened with syrup, in the bottom of each individual mold.
Fill to the top with cherry bavarian cream and add cooked cherries in the center.
Smooth the top of the mold with a metal spatula and place in the freezer for about 2 hours to set.
Make the chocolate disks, the white chocolate fans and the cherry coulis.

Plate Presentation
Brush the tops of the chilled desserts with melted red currant jelly.
Remove the rings and press the chocolate disks on the sides.
Ladle cherry sauce on one side of the plate and decorate the dessert with fans of white chocolate and cooked (or fresh) cherries.

Jelly glaze

Sliced cherries

Chocolate sponge cake with marascino syrup

Marascino bavarian cream

Pineapple Meringue Tart

This tart combines the tropical flavors of coconut, rum, and pineapple. The meringue on the top is shaped and browned to resemble the covering of a pineapple.

Ingredients

Sweet pie pastry
Coconut sponge cake
Sugar syrup with rum
Pineapple filling
Italian meringue

Procedure

Line the pastry rings (7 cm (3 in)) with sweet pie pastry.
Prick with a fork and bake at 200 C (400 F) 8-10 minutes.
Cut circles of sponge cake a little smaller than the rings and moisten with rum syrup.
Make the pineapple filling and the Italian meringue.

Plate Presentation

Trim the baked pastry with a small knife.
Place the moistened cake circles in the bottom of the baked pastries.
Mound the pineapple cream in the mold using a small spatula.
Pipe Italian meringue (7 mm (1/4 in) tip) over the pineapple cream, drawing the tip straight up to form little points over the surface.
Place in a hot oven for a few seconds to brown the meringue.
Place in the center of the serving plate.

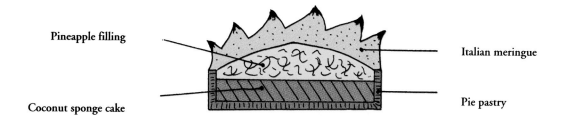

Pineapple filling

Coconut sponge cake

Italian meringue

Pie pastry

81

"Africa"

Although the hexagonal mold used here makes a stunning presentation, a high-sided pastry ring in any shape can be used. The components of this dessert come from warm climates: coconut, pineappple, rum vanilla and chocolate.

Ingredients

Coconut sponge cake	*Decoration:*
Rum-flavored sugar syrup	Chocolate glaze
Chocolate mousse	Candied pineapple
Vanilla bavarian	Two-toned cigarettes
Pineapple filling	White chocolate disks
Apricot jelly glaze	Chocolate curls

Procedure

Place a layer of coconut sponge cake in the bottom of the molds and moisten with rum syrup. Pipe a layer of chocolate mousse on top of the cake then a layer of pineapple cream. Finish with a layer of vanilla bavarian cream. Smooth the top with a metal spatula and place in the freezer about 2 hours to set.
Prepare the chocolate curls, the cigarettes, the white chocolate disks and the candied pineapple.

Plate Presentation

Brush apricot glaze on the top of the chilled dessert.
Remove the mold and place on the plate.
Decorate the plate with jelly glaze and chocolate glaze piped through a paper cone.
Garnish with the candied pineapple, chocolate curls, cigarettes and white chocolate disks.

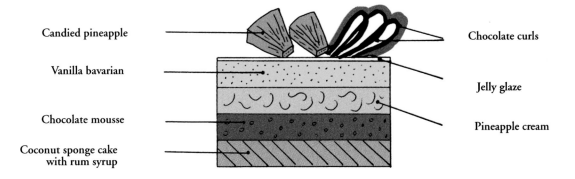

Candied pineapple

Vanilla bavarian

Chocolate mousse

Coconut sponge cake
with rum syrup

Chocolate curls

Jelly glaze

Pineapple cream

Chocolate Triangles with Cherries

The cherries used here are called "Amaréna" which have a rich flavor and texture. Use the best preserved cherries you can find for this elegant dessert.

Ingredients

Chocolate triangles
Chocolate mousse
Cooked cherries

Decoration:
Chocolate curls

Sauce:
Sabayon with Kirsch

Procedure

Form a thin sheet (1 mm (1/20 in) of tempered covering chocolate and cut the triangles from the cooled chocolate.
For a fancier presentation, one of triangles can be made from a striped sheet of chocolate.
Make the chocolate mousse and fold in cherries.
Make the sabayon with Kirsch and the chocolate curls.

Plate Presentation

Alternate dollops of chocolate mousse with cherries and the chocolate triangles.
Spoon a little sabayon with Kirsch on the plate and decorate with chocolate curls.

Chocolate mousse — Striped chocolate triangle

Cherries — Chocolate triangle

Babas with Grapes and Muscat Sabayon

The "Muscat" used to soak the babas and make the sabayon is a fruity wine that marries well with the fresh grape garnish. When the same batter is baked in a ring mold, it is called a "savarin".

Ingredients

Dough for "babas" or savarin
Vanilla pastry cream
White seedless grapes
Apple jelly or apricot jam
  (for glaze)

Decoration:
Nougatine triangles
White raisins, macerated

Sauce:
Sabayon with Muscat

Procedure

Bake the dough in the traditional high-sided "baba" molds at 200 C (400 F).
Cool the cakes then soak in light syrup (500 g (1 lb) sugar, 1 L (1 qt) water, zest of 1 lemon, 1 vanilla bean (split)). The babas should be thoroughly soaked with syrup. When they have absorbed the syrup, remove the babas with a slotted spoon and place on a cooling rack.
Sprinkle the warm cakes with Muscat and cool.
Make the nougatine garnish and peel the grapes.
Make the vanilla pastry cream and Muscat sabayon.

Plate Presentation

Just before serving, sprinkle a little more Muscat over the babas. Cut the cakes in half and spread pastry cream on the inside and garnish with grapes.
Brush apricot glaze on the outside of the baba and place on the plate. Spoon sabayon on the plate and garnish with nougatine and macerated raisins.

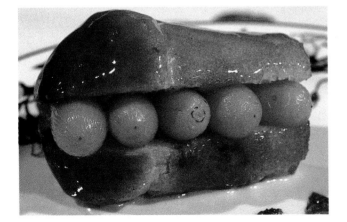

Apricot glaze

Vanilla pastry cream

Baba with Muscat

Peeled grapes

Chocolate Leaves with Grapes

Whipped cream and grapes form the filling between thin layers of bittersweet chocolate. The deep color and flavor of the black raspberry sauce set off this light dessert.

Ingredients

Chocolate disks
Whipped cream
White grapes

Sauce:
Black raspberry coulis

Procedure

For each serving, make three large disks of bittersweet covering chocolate.
Make the black raspberry coulis and peel the grapes.
Shortly before serving, whip the cream in a cold bowl.

Plate Presentation

Pipe a dollop of whipped cream in the center of a chocolate disk. Arrange peeled grapes around the cream.
Place a second disk on top, pipe more cream and add grapes and finish with a chocolate disk on top.
Spoon the black raspberry coulis on the plate and garnish with 2 grapes.

Chocolate disk

Whipped cream

Raisin

Peeled green grapes

Pineapple "Pavé" with Mango Coulis

The assembled dessert is dipped in tempered chocolate for a stunning presentation.

Ingredients

Rum buttercream
Genoise
Rum-flavored sugar syrup
Pineapple filling
Covering chocolate

Jelly glaze
Chocolate glaze
Decoration:
Candied pineapple
Sauce:
Mango coulis

Procedure

Cover the sides of small rectangular molds with a thin layer of rum-flavored buttercream. Place a rectangle of genoise into the bottom of the mold and moisten with rum syrup. Add a layer of pineapple cream and top with another layer of imbibed cake. Add buttercream to the top of the mold and smooth the surface with a metal spatula. Refrigerate to firm the buttercream. Make the candied pineapple and mango coulis.

Plate Presentation

When the buttercream is set, unmold the dessert. Retun to the refrigerator to chill thoroughly.
Temper a small pot of covering chocolate and dip the chilled "pavés" about halfway in the melted chocolate.
When the chocolate has set, place the dessert on the plate.
Garnish the top of the rectangle with candied pineapple and brush with glaze. Pipe the mango coulis through a paper cone in a decorative design on the plate.

Candied pineapple

Genoise with
rum syrup

Pineapple filling

Jelly glaze

Covering chocolate

Rum buttercream

Introduction **Tropical Fruits**

Desserts made with tropical fruits are as colorful as they are delicious. Slice the fruits carefully to make the most of the interesting shapes. Star fruit, kiwi, mango, passion fruit, banana and pineapple are festive ingredients for desserts.

1. "Ile Maurice"

2. Savarin with Tropical Fruits"

3. Mango Mousse with Tropical Fruits

4. Frozen Nougat Creole

5. Tropical Fruit Sorbet

"L'Ile Maurice"

"L'Ile Maurice", off the eastern coast of Africa is a favorite vacation spot for the French. The sun-drenched fruits of this island paradise come together in this combination of mango and passion fruit mousse with coconut cake imbibed with rum.

Ingredients

Mango mousse	*Decoration:*
Passion fruit mousse	Tropical fruits
Coconut sponge cake	Mint leaves
Almond sponge cake (striped)	Chocolate decoration
Rum-flavored sugar syrup	Chocolate glaze
Jelly glaze	***Sauce:***
	Mango coulis

Procedure

Wrap a strip of the striped almond sponge cake (cut to go 2/3 the way up the mold) around the inside of the ring molds. (A tear drop-shaped mold is used here, but any high-sided, bottomless pastry ring can be used.) Place a layer of coconut sponge cake in the bottom and moisten with rum syrup.
Fill the mold halfway with mango mousse and place in the freezer 1/2 hour to set. Add passion fruit mousse and smooth the top with a metal spatula. Place in the freezer about 2 hours to set. Make the chocolate decorations, chocolate glaze, the mango coulis and prepare the tropical fruits.

Plate Presentation

Carefully brush melted jelly glaze on the top of the chilled desserts. Remove the pastry ring and place on the plate.
Garnish with tropical fruits and chocolate decorations.
Pipe the mango sauce and chocolate glaze around the dessert in a decorative design with a paper cone.

Jelly glaze

Striped almond
sponge cake

Coconut sponge cake
with rum syrup

Chocolate decoration

Passion fruit mousse

Mango mousse

Savarin
with Tropical Fruits

The rum soaked savarin cake is the perfect base for the colorful and intensely-flavored tropical fruits. Savarins are often made in a large ring mold with a mound of fruit in the center but these individual savarins make a stunning plate presentation.

Ingredients

"Baba" dough
Light sugar syrup
Rum
Jelly glaze

Decoration:
Tropical fruits

Sauce:
Coconut sauce

Procedure

Fill individual ring molds halfway with the baba dough, let rise according to directions and bake at 200 C (400 F) until puffed and golden. Unmold and transfer to a cooling rack.
Immerse the cooled savarins in light sugar syrup (500 g (1 lb sugar), 1 L (1 qt) water, zest of 1 lemon, 1 split vanilla bean). When the cakes are thoroughly soaked, transfer to a cooling rack to drain excess syrup and sprinkle with rum.
Prepare the tropical fruits and make the coconut sauce.

Plate Presentation

Just before serving, sprinkle the cake with rum. Brush the top of the savarins with jelly glaze and place in the center of the plate. In the center of the cakes, arrange one piece of each fruit in an attractive pattern and spoon coconut sauce around the cake.

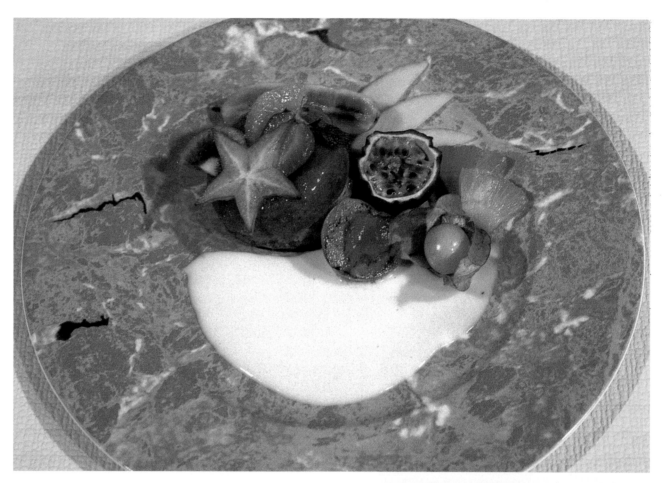

89

Mango Mousse
with Tropical Fruits

A colorful array of tropical fruits top a delicate mango mousse which served with a bright, flavorful passion fruit sauce. Rum-soaked cake and chocolate decorations finish this pretty dessert.

Ingredients

Mango mousse
Genoise
Sugar syrup with rum
Cocoa powder
Jelly glaze

Decoration:
Tropical fruits
Chocolate disks

Sauce:
Passion fruit sauce

Procedure

Place a layer of genoise in the bottom of each mold and moisten with rum-flavored syrup. Fill with mango mousse and smooth the top with a metal spatula.
Place in the freezer about 2 hours to set.
Make the chocolate disks, prepare the tropical fruits and make the passion fruit sauce.

Plate Presentation

Sprinkle the top of the chilled dessert with cocoa powder.
Very carefully, add melted jelly glaze to the top.
Remove the mold, place on the plate and press the chocolate disks to the sides. Decorate with the fruits.

Genoise with
rum syrup

Jelly glaze with
cocoa powder

Mango mousse

Frozen Nougat Creole

Nougat candy is a traditional French sweet that has been transformed into a luscious frozen dessert. Honey, macerated raisins, and caramelized almonds flavor this creamy meringue. The tartness of the mango coulis adds just the right touch.

Ingredients

Frozen nougat creole

Decoration:
Chocolate disks
Tropical fruits

Sauce:
Mango coulis

Procedure

Line a cylindrical mold with plastic wrap.

Make the honey-based nougat mixture with rum-macerated raisins and caramelized almonds (chopped).

Fill the mold to the top with the nougat, cover and place in freezer for 2 hours or until frozen.

Make the mango coulis, the chocolate disks and prepare the tropical fruits.

Plate Presentation

Unmold the nougat «log» and cut three slices of 1.5 cm (about 1/2 in)) for each serving.

Alternate the slices of nougat with the chocolate disks.

Garnish the plate with slices of tropical furits and spoon the mango coulis around the dessert.

Tropical Fruit Sorbets

In French restaurants, sorbets are often arranged on a plate with cookies and fruits to make a special dessert.

Ingredients

Filo sheets
Unsalted butter, melted
Coconut sorbet
Mango sorbet
Decoration:
Tropical fruits
Sauce:
Passion fruit sauce

Plate Presentation

On the serving plate, alternate three scoops of sorbet with crispy pastry triangles.

Garnish with tropical fruits and spoon passion fruit sauce around the dessert.

Procedure

Cut each sheet of filo dough into large triangles.

Brush both sides of the dough with melted butter and bake at 375 F a minute or two until golden and crispy.

Make the coconut and mango sorbets, prepare the tropical fruits and make the passion fruit sauce.

Chapter 4 - Desserts Made with Winter Fruits, Dried Fruits and Nuts

Introduction **Bananas, Kiwis and Prunes**

Use perfectly ripe bananas for best results. Tiny bananas, found at specialty shops, are the sweetest.

Kiwis need to be very ripe and soft when used as a filling but slightly firmer when being sliced for decoration. Once an exotic and expensive fruit, kiwis are now cultivated in many countries and are available and affordable year round.

For the French, the moist, meaty prunes from "Agen" are the best. To augment their flavor, they are traditionally macerated in Armagnac.

1. **Banana Dome**
2. **Banana Gratin**
3. **Caramelized Bananas with Rum Sabayon and Coconut Sorbet**
4. **Pear and Kiwi Mousse**
5. **Kiwi and Frozen Coconut Mousse with Raspberry Caramel Sauce**
6. **Kiwi Tart**
7. **Prune Tart**
8. **"Far Breton"**
9. **Armagnac Parfait with Prune Coulis**

Banana Dome

This dramtic white and dark chocolate dome encloses chocolate mousse with banana slices. A crispy base of hazelnut meringue and a colorful mango coulis complete the dessert.

Ingredients

White chocolate domes
  with dark chocolate
  decoration
Chocolate mousse
Banana slices
Rum
Hazelnut meringue
  ("dacquoise")

Decoration:
Banana slices
Two-toned cigarettes
Chocolate disks

Sauce:
Mango coulis

Procedure

The white covering chocolate shell should be made as thin as possible so the dessert is not difficult to eat. The dark covering chocolate is sprayed through a special pistol to achieve the splattering effect.

Fill the chocolate domes with chocolate mousse with slices of bananas (baked with sugar in the oven then flamed with rum). Cut a circle of baked hazelnut meringue (dacquoise) to cover the base of the dome. Refrigerate 1/2 hour.

Make the mango coulis, cigarettes, and chocolate disks.

Plate Presentation

Unmold the chilled chocolate dome and place in the center of the serving plate.

With a paper cone, pipe a decorative design with the mango coulis. Garnish the plate with flambéed banana slices, a cigarette and a chocolate disk.

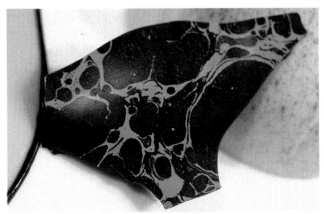

White and Dark Chocolate Dome

Hazelnut meringue

Chocolate mousse with baked banana slices

Chocolate mousse

Banana Gratin

Rum-macerated raisins are combined with bananas and covered with a rich creamy sacue that browns beautifully under the broiler.

Ingredients

Bananas
Raisins, macerated in rum
Gratin mixture

Procedure

Peel the bananas then cut lengthwise.
Bake in the oven with butter and sugar then flambée with rum.
Macerate the raisins and make the gratin mixture.

Plate Presentation

Place the bananas and macerated raisins in the gratin dish and cover with gratin mixture.
Place under the broiler 1-2 minutes until the top is evenly browned.
Flame with rum and serve at once.

Caramelized Bananas with Rum Sabayon and Coconut Sorbet

A beautiful dessert of warm flambéed bananas with a refreshing coconut sorbet. Rum-macerated raisins and a rum sabayon set off this exotic dessert.

Ingredients

Small bananas
Coconut sorbet

Decoration:
Raisins macerated in rum

Sauce:
Rum sabayon

Procedure

Make the coconut sorbet and macerate the raisins in rum.
Cut the small bananas in half lengthwise.
Bake the bananas in a hot oven with sugar and butter until caramelized, flambée with rum.
Make the rum sabayon.

Plate Presentation

Fan out the bananas on the plate and place a scoop of coconut sorbet in the center.
Spoon a little rum sabayon between the bananas.
Garnish with rum-macerated raisins.
Serve at once.

Pear and Kiwi Mousse

Chocolate sponge cake separates layers of pear mousse and kiwi mousse, served with matching sauces of pear and kiwi.

Ingredients

Pear Mousse
Kiwi Mousse
Chocolate sponge cake
Rum-flavored sugar syrup

Sauces:
Pear coulis
Kiwi coulis

Decoration:
Jelly glaze
Kiwi slices
Chocolate disks

Procedure

In the base of individual oval molds, place a layer of chocolate sponge cake moistened with rum syrup. Add a layer of pear mousse, a layer of moistened sponge cake then fill with kiwi mousse. Smooth the top with a metal spatula. Place in freezer 2 hours to set.
Peel and slice the kiwis, make the chocolate decorations and make the two coulis.

Plate Presentation

Brush the top of the chilled desserts with jelly glaze.
Remove the molds and place on the serving plates.
Press the chocolate disks on the sides and garnish with kiwi slices. Spoon a little of each coulis on the plate.

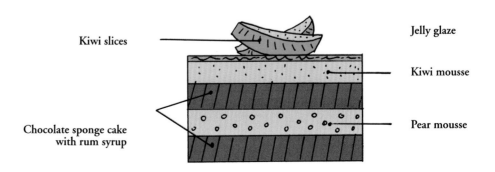

Kiwi slices — Jelly glaze

Kiwi mousse

Chocolate sponge cake with rum syrup — Pear mousse

Kiwi with Frozen Coconut Mousse and Raspberry Caramel Sauce

Kiwi slices garnish a plate with frozen coconut mousse and a rich raspberry caramel sauce that adds just the right flavor and color accent. If dome-shaped molds are not available, use another individual mold or the mousse can be frozen in a shallow dish and scooped.

Ingredients

Kiwis
Frozen coconut mousse

Decoration:
Fresh mint leaves

Sauce:
Raspberry caramel sauce

Procedure

Fill dome-shaped molds with coconut mousse.
Place in the freezer for 2 hours.
Peel and cut the kiwis in slices then cut the slices in half.
Make the raspberry caramel sauce.

Plate Presentation

Unmold the frozen coconut mousse onto the serving plate.
Fan out the overlapping semi-circles of kiwi around the dome.
Spoon a little raspberry caramel sauce around the mousse.

Kiwi Tart

Kiwi slices replace pear slices in the classic French almond tart. The raspberry preserves add contrast of color and flavor.

Ingredients

Sweet pie pastry
Raspberry preserves
Almond cream
Kiwis
Jelly glaze

Decoration:
Strawberries

Procedure

Press circles of sweet pie pastry into 7 cm (3 in) pastry rings.
Spread a thin layer of raspberry preserves in the bottom and cover with a layer of almond cream.
Bake in a preheated 200 C (400 F) oven for about 20 minutes or until the pastry is golden and the almond cream is set.
Remove the pastry rings and place the tarts on a cooling rack.
Trim the edges of the baked pastry.
Peel and slice the kiwis.

Plate Presentation

Just before serving, overlap the slices of kiwi in a circle on the tart.
Brush the top with jelly glaze and place on the plate.
Garnish the top with half a strawberry and brush with glaze.

Prune Tart

Prunes in Armagnac are a specialty in France that add a wonderful flavor to this tart of puréed prunes and almond cream.

Ingredients

Sweet pie pastry
Prune purée
Almond cream
Red currant jelly glaze

Decoration:
Prunes in Armagnac
Fresh mint leaves

Sauce:
Vanilla crème anglaise

Procedure

Line the pastry rings (7 cm (3 in)) with sweet pie pastry.
Fill halfway with prune purée then pipe almond cream to the top.
Bake in a preheated 200 C (400 F) oven about 20 minutes, until the pastry is golden and the almond cream in set.
Remove the rings, place on a cooling rack and trim the edges of the pastry.
Make the crème anglaise.
Drain the prunes, remove the pits and cut in half.

Plate Presentation

Brush with jelly glaze and arrange prunes on top of the tart.
Spoon crème anglaise on the plate and place the tart in the center.
Garnish with prunes and mint leaves.

Red currant jelly glaze

Prune purée

Mint leaf

Prunes in Armagnac

Almond cream

Sweet pie pastry

Far Breton

This rustic specialty from Brittany in western France is a simple-to-make flan with prunes.
In this adaptation, the «Far» is served with crème anglaise and a prune coulis. It remains an informal dish that would be an ideal luncheon dessert.

Ingredients

Prunes in Armagnac
"Far" mixture

Sauces:
Crème anglaise
Prune coulis

Procedure

Butter a shallow earthenware baking dish.
Place several prunes in the bottom and fill 3/4 full with the Far mixture.
Bake at 200 C (400 F) for 30-45 minutes (depending on the size of the dish), until set and lightly browned on the top. Set aside to cool.
Make the crème anglaise and the prune coulis.

Plate Presentation

Place a portion of the "Far Breton" on the plate and spoon crème anglaise and prune coulis on the side.

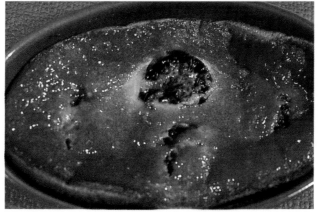

Armagnac Parfait with Prune Coulis

In France, "parfait" is a rich frozen dessert made with eggs, cooked sugar and cream and formed in a decorative mold. The delicate leaf-shaped wafers are made from the classic "cat's tongue"(langue de chat) batter that can also be formed in rolled "cigarettes" or formed while still warm to make a "tulip".

Ingredients

Parfait mixture with Armagnac
Covering chocolate, melted

Decoration:
Leaf-shaped cookies
Two-toned cigarettes
Chocolate decorations
Prunes in Armagnac

Sauce:
Prune coulis

Procedure

Fill individual dome-shaped molds with the parfait mixture.
Place in the freezer 2 hours.
Make the prune coulis, cookie leaves, cigarettes and chocolate decor.

Plate Presentation

Unmold the frozen parfait.
Make a decorative design with melted covering chocolate by drizzling with a spoon or using a "patissier's pistolet" to direct the stream of chocolate in a decorative pattern.
Place the cookie leaves around the parfait.
Garnish with the cigarettes and chocolate decorations.
Spoon a little prune coulis on the plate and add a few macerated prunes.

Introduction
Chestnuts

French chestnut purée, available in cans, is a delicious ingredient that is easy to use. Vanilla brings out the subtle flavor of the chestnuts in a variety of desserts. One small region, the "Ardèche", produces one quarter of all the chestnuts in France.

1. "Bûche Solognaate"

2. Chestnut Mice

3. Chestnut Ice cream

"Bûche Solognote"

Yule log-shaped cakes («bûches») are the traditional dessert for Christmas eve in France and candied chestnuts (a specialty of the Sologne region) are also a favorite treat at this time of year. In this "bûche", almond sponge cake is filled with chestnut bavarian cream.

Ingredients

Almond sponge cake
Hazelnut meringue
   ("dacquoise")
Rum-flavored sugar syrup
Chestnut bavarian cream
Candied chestnuts
Chocolate glaze

Decoration:
Chocolate twigs
Two-toned cigarettes
Candied chestnuts

Sauce:
Rum sabayon

Procedure

Line a cylindrical mold with plastic wrap then with a sheet of almond sponge cake, moistened with rum syrup. Fill the mold with chestnut bavarian, adding chopped candied chestnuts throughout. Place a rectangle of hazelnut meringue on the top, cover and place in the freezer for about 2 hours to set.
Remove the chilled "bûche" from the mold and coat the sponge cake with chocolate glaze.
Cut a thin slice off each end for a neat appearance.
Make the rum sabayon.

Plate Presentation

Cut two 1 inch slices and arrange them on the serving plate. Spoon the rum sabayon around the slices and garnish with chocolate twigs and candied chestnuts.

Chocolate glaze

Chestnut bavarian

Hazelnut meringue

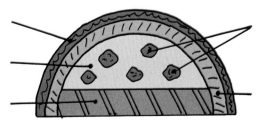

Chopped candied chestnuts

Almond sponge cake
with rum syrup

Chestnut Mice

Chestnut buttercream is piped out to resemble mice, coated in chocolate and served with crème anglaise. A fun and tasty dessert for children of all ages.

Ingredients

Sweet pie pastry
Almond cream
Chestnut buttercream
Covering chocolate

Sauce:
Vanilla crème anglaise

Decoration:

Royal icing
Chocolate glaze
Sliced almonds
Chocolate curls
Marzipan "cheese"

Procedure

Brush butter on boat-shaped molds and line with sweet pie pastry.
Fill the mold to the top with almond cream.
Chill for 30 minutes then bake in a preheated 200 C (400 F) oven about 15 minutes. Cool and remove the molds.
Using a plain 15 mm (about 1/2 in) tip, pipe mouse-shaped dollops of chestnut buttercream on each little tart. Place sliced almonds on top for "ears" and chill in the freezer 1/2 hour.
Temper the covering chocolate and coat the chilled mice.
Use a paper cone filled with royal icing to pipe "eyes", "nose" and a "tail" on the mice.
Make the vanilla crème anglaise.
Form small pieces of marzipan into «cheeses» for each plate.

Plate Presentation

Place two mice on a plate with a little crème anglaise, a marzipan cheese and a few chocolate curls

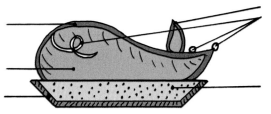

Covering chocolate

Chestnut buttercream

Sweet pie pastry

Sliced almond «ears»

Eyes, nose and tail made with royal icing

Almond cream

107

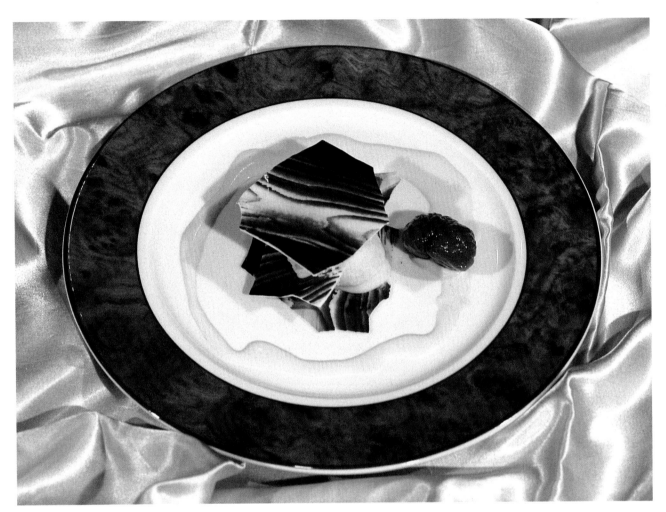

Chestnut Ice Cream

Gathering chestnuts in the woods is a favorite pastime in France so chocolate, shaped like bark, is the perfect decoration for this dessert of candied chestnut ice cream.

Ingredients

Covering chocolate
Chestnut ice cream

Decoration:
Jelly glaze
Covering chocolate (white and dark)
Chocolate curls
Peeled pistachios
Candied chestnuts

Sauces:
Pistachio crème anglaise
Rum sabayon

Procedure

Marble the two covering chocolates and form irregular, bark-like pieces.
Make the candied chestnut ice cream.
Peel the pistachios.
Make the pistachio crème anglaise and the rum sabayon.

Plate Presentation

Place three scoops of chestnut ice cream on the plate with chocolate bark in between. Spoon the two sauces around the ice cream, garnish with pistachios and a candied chestnut and decorate the plate with jelly glaze.

Introduction
Pistachios and Hazelnuts

Pistachios and hazelnuts are used in many French pastries. The shells and skins are removed and the nuts are toasted or caramelized to intensify their flavor. They can be ground and used in fillings and also used whole as decorations. Peeled pistachios keep well in the freezer. When flavoring a creamy mixture, French pastry chefs traditionally use an unsweetened nut paste, available in cans.

1. Pistachio Bavarian Cream

2. Nut Lover's Dream

3. Pistachio Tuiles with Caramelized Apricots

4. Pistachio "Pavé" with Three Sauces

5. "Le Piémontais"

6. Squirrel's Delight

Pistachio Bavarian Cream

Pistachio bavarian is paired with a vanilla bavarian, layered with chocolate sponge cake and served with a pistachio crème anglaise. The striped almond sponge cake around the sides

Ingredients

Almond sponge cake
Chocolate sponge cake'
Vanilla-flavored sugar syrup
Pistachio bavarian cream
Jelly glaze

Decoration:
Marbled chocolate disks
Chocolate curls
Pistachios, peeled

Sauce:
Pistachio crème anglaise

Procedure

Line individual molds (2/3 the way up the sides) with strips of striped almond sponge cake.
Place a layer of chocolate sponge cake in the bottom and moisten with vanilla syrup.
Fill halfway with vanilla bavarian and place in the freezer 1/2 hour to firm up.
Fill to the top with pistachio bavarian and smooth the top with a metal spatula. Place in the freezer about 2 hours to set.
Make the pistachio crème anglaise, the marbled chocolate disks and the chocolate curls.

Plate Presentation

Brush the top of the chilled desserts with jelly glaze.
Unmold and place on the plates.
Spoon pistachio crème anglaise on the plate and garnish with peeled pistachios and the chocolate decorations.

Jelly glaze

Pistachios

Pistachio bavarian

Vanilla bavarian

Almond sponge cake

Chocolate sponge cake
with vanilla syrup

Nut Lovers' Dream

This "woodsy" dessert combines hazelnut, pistachio and almond with Kirsch and chocolate.

Ingredients

Hazelnut meringue
  («dacquoise»)
Pistachio bavarian cream
Hazelnut mousse
Almond sponge cake
Sugar syrup with Kirsch
Jelly glaze
Coffee syrup

Decoration:
Two-toned chocolate ciga-
  rettes
Chocolate twigs
Hazelnuts, peeled and toas-
  ted
Sauce:
Hazelnut caramel sauce

Procedure

Fill each round, high-sided pastry ring with the following layers: a circle of hazelnut meringue, a layer of pistachio bavarian, a circle of almond sponge cake moistened with Kirsch syrup. Fill with a layer of hazelnut moussse and smooth the top.
Place in the freezer for about 2 hours to set.
Make a hazelnut caramel sauce, chocolate twigs, and two-toned chocolate cigarettes.

Plate Presentation

Glaze the top of the chilled desserts with jelly glaze swirled with coffee syrup.
Remove the mold and place on the plate.
Press the chocolate twigs around the sides and pipe the caramel sauce around the dessert in a decorative pattern with a paper cone.
Garnish with chocolate cigarettes and toasted hazelnuts.

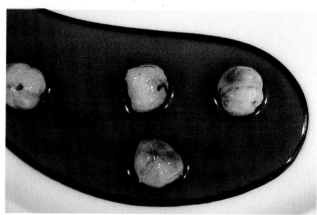

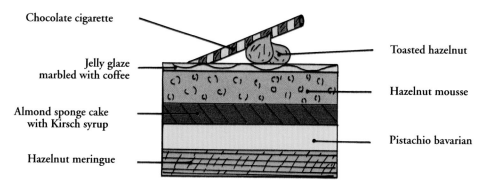

Chocolate cigarette

Jelly glaze
marbled with coffee

Almond sponge cake
with Kirsch syrup

Hazelnut meringue

Toasted hazelnut

Hazelnut mousse

Pistachio bavarian

Pistachios "Tuiles" with Caramelized Apricots

"Tuiles" or "tile" cookies are so named because they are shaped to resemble the curved terra cotta tiles on the houses of southern France. These delicate cookies can be made with any nut and are delicious on their own.

Ingredients

Pistachio «tuiles»
Pistachio pastry cream
Apricot halves, caramelized

Decoration:
Pistachios
Chocolate disks

Sauce:
Apricot caramel sauce

Procedure

Make the cookies, using coarsely chopped pistachios.
Make pastry cream with an addition of pistachio butter then fold in whipped cream to lighten it.

Make the chocolate disks, blanch the pistachios and remove the skins, caramelize the apricots and make the apricot caramel sauce.

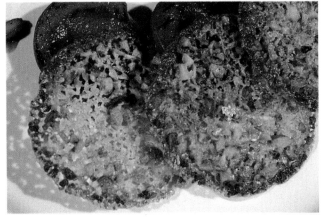

Plate Presentation

On each plate, alternate three cookies with three spoonfuls of pistachio cream. Add three caramelized apricot halves and spoon sauce around the dessert.

Garnish with pistachios and chocolate disks.

Pistachio "Pavé"
with Three Sauces

The top layer of sponge cake is decorated with a wood grain design which is made with a special stencil.

Ingredients

Almond sponge cake
Sugar syrup with Kirsch
Covering chocolate
Pistachio bavarian cream
Jelly glaze

Decoration:
Chocolate curls
Pistachios
Chocolate glaze

Sauces:
Vanilla crème anglaise
Coffee crème anglaise
Chocolate sauce

Procedure

Temper covering chocolate and coat one side of a rectangle of sponge cake (cut to fit in the mold). When the chocolate is set, turn it over and lay it on the bottom of the mold and moisten with Kirsch syrup.
Fill almost to the top of the mold with pistachio bavarian and cover with another layer of imbibed sponge cake.
Cover and freeze for about 2 hours to set.
Make the chocolate curls and the three sauces.

Plate Presentation

Slice the chilled dessert from the end to make rectangles 7 cm X 5 cm (3 in X 2 in). Coat the top with jelly glaze and place on the plate.
Use a paper cone to pipe the three sauces on the plate in a decorative design.
Garnish with pistachios and chocolate curls.

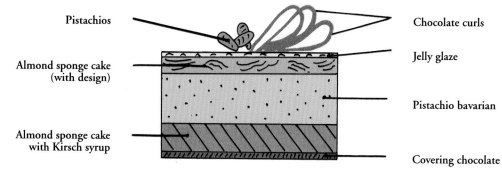

Pistachios — Almond sponge cake (with design) — Almond sponge cake with Kirsch syrup — Chocolate curls — Jelly glaze — Pistachio bavarian — Covering chocolate

"Le Piémontais"

This dessert is named for the Piedmont region in northern Italy, well-known for its delicious hazelnuts which are featured in this dessert.

Ingredients

Hazelnut "dacquoise"
  (meringue)
Covering chocolate
Hazelnut buttercream

Decoration:
Marbled chocolate disks
Toasted hazelnuts

Sauces:
Caramel sauce
Vanilla crème anglaise

Procedure

Spread tempered covering chocolate on the bottom of one of the meringue rectangles and cool to set. Layer hazelnut buttercream between three layers of baked hazelnut meringue. Cover the top with buttercream, smooth the surface and place in freezer 30 minutes.
Make the marbled chocolate disks, the caramel sauce and the crème anglaise. Toast the hazelnuts to loosen the skins, rub off the skins then return the nuts to the oven to toast to a golden brown.

Plate Presentation

The top of the chilled dessert can be decorated with tempered chocolate "shot" from a special pastry "pistol".
Cut the rectangle into triangles.
Place on the plate with the two sauces.
Garnish with the chocolate disks and toasted hazelnuts.

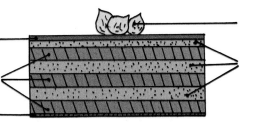

Chocolate disk

Hazelnut meringue

Covering chocolate

Toasted hazelnuts

Hazelnut buttercream

Squirrels' Delight

Hazelnuts impart a luscious flavor to ice cream which is combined here with almond brittle ("nougatine"), chocolate and caramel sauce.

Ingredients

Hazelnut ice cream
Nougatine triangles
Chocolate triangles

Decoration:
Toasted hazelnuts

Sauce:
Caramel sauce

Procedure

Make the chocolate triangles (for a fancy touch, add stripes of white chocolate).
To toast hazelnuts (for ice cream and garnish) place nuts in a single layer on a baking sheet, place in medium-hot oven to loosen the skins. Rub off the skins with a towel then return skinnned nuts to the oven to toast.
Make the hazelnut ice cream.
Make the nougatine triangles and caramel sauce.

Plate Presentation

Make three "quenelles" of ice cream (formed with two soup spoons dipped in hot water) and alternate them on the plate with the chocolate triangles.
Ladle caramel sauce on the plate and garnish with the nougatine triangles and toasted hazelnuts.

115

Introduction
Walnuts and Almonds

Walnuts are used whole, chopped, ground, or in a paste. The skin tends to give a bitter taste, so use the best quality walnuts available. Almonds are a basic ingredient in French pastry kitchens and are used to flavor many preparations: spongecakes, creams, fillings, pastry dough, and are used in many forms as a decoration.

It is recommended to buy almonds packaged in 2 lbs containers and to not store them for too long a time as they will become rancid.

1. "Délice du Perigord"
2. "Sarlat"
3. "Amandine"
4. "Blanc-Manger"
5. "Duglesclin"
6. Walnut Ice Cream with "Croustillants"

"Délice du Perigord"

The best walnuts in France come from the Perigord region. In addition to the walnut cream, this dessert features a walnut brittle or "nougatine" and a jelly glaze with walnut flavoring.

Ingredients

Biscuit russe
Walnut cream
Walnut nougatine
Covering chocolate
Walnut-flavored jelly glaze
Coffee syrup

Decoration:
Chocolate disks
Walnut halves

Sauce:
Vanilla crème anglaise

Procedure

Cut three rectangles of cake to fit the mold.
Spread one layer with tempered covering chocolate and place it, chocolate side down, in the bottom of the mold.
Add two layers of walnut cream between layers of cake and finish with walnut cream in a smooth layer on the top.
Cover and place in the freezer about 30 minutes to set.
Make the vanilla crème anglaise, walnut glaze, and the chocolate decorations.

Plate Presentation

When the dessert is set, cut into triangular individual portions.
Coat the top with walnut glaze and place two triangles on each plate.
Garnish with the chocolate disks and walnut halves.
Spoon crème anglaise on the plate and swirl with coffee syrup.

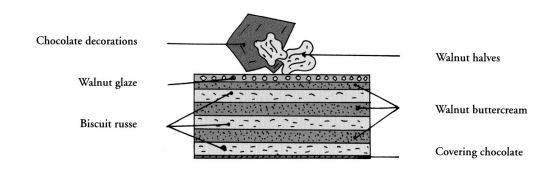

Chocolate decorations

Walnut glaze

Biscuit russe

Walnut halves

Walnut buttercream

Covering chocolate

117

"Sarlat"

Sarlat is a city in the southwest region of France where top-quality walnuts are found. Here, walnut bavarian is combined with walnut brittle ("nougatine") and chocolate sponge cake is imbibed with walnut syrup.

Ingredients

Walnut bavarian cream
Almond meringue ("succès")
Chocolate sponge cake
Sugar syrup with walnut flavoring
Walnut brittle, crumbled

Decoration:
Walnut halves
Walnut brittle rectangles
Chocolate disks

Sauce:
Caramel sauce

Procedure

Fill each individual mold with the following layers: almond meringue on the bottom, a layer of walnut bavarian, a circle of chocolate sponge cake moistened with walnut-flavored syrup, then add bavarian cream and smooth the top.
Place in the freezer for about 2 hours to set.
Make the walnut brittle ("nougatine"), shaping some into rectangles and crumbling the rest.
Make the chocolate disks and the caramel sauce.

Plate Presentation

When the dessert is set, cover the top with crumbled nougatine.
Remove the molds and place on the plate.
Press the chocolate disks on the sides and spoon the caramel sauce on the plate. Garnish with nougatine rectangles and walnut halves.

Nougatine, crumbled

Walnut bavarian

Chocolate sponge cake

Almond meringue

118

"Amandine"

"Amandine", a bite-size tart of sweet pie pastry and almond cream filling, is a classic offering in French pastry shops. Here the basic tart is augmented with a layer of raspberry jam and served with a raspberry sauce ("coulis").

Ingredients

Sweet pie pastry
Raspberry jam
Almond cream
Sliced almonds

Decoration:
Jelly glaze

Sauce:
Raspberry coulis

Procedure

Press cirlces of sweet pie pastry into 7 cm (3 in) pastry rings.
Spread a thin layer of raspberry jam in the bottom then pipe almond cream to the top of the mold and arrange sliced almonds on top.
Bake in a preheated oven 200 C (440 F) for about 20 minutes.
Remove the rings, place on a cooling rack and trim the edges of the pastry.
Make the raspberry coulis.

Plate Presentation

Brush the jelly glaze on top of each tart.
Coat the bottom of the plate with raspberry coulis and place the tart in the center.

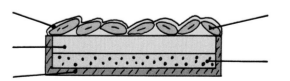

Jelly glaze

Almond cream

Sweet pie pastry

Sliced almonds

Raspberry jam

"Blanc-Manger"

"Blanc-manger", a French dessert that dates to Medieval times, is updated here with crispy puff pastry and a raspberry sauce. The combination of fruits can vary according to availability.

Ingredients

Blanc-manger mixture
Puff pastry
Red fruits

Decoration:
Red fruits
Chocolate disks

Sauce:
Raspberry coulis

Procedure

Make the blanc-manger mixture, pour into dome-shaped molds and place in the freezer about 2 hours or until set.
Wash the fruits (strawberries, raspberries, currants), then cook them over low heat with a little butter and sugar.
Make the chocolate disks and raspberry coulis.
Cut the pastry into teardrop shapes, brush with egg glaze, score the top with the tip of a small knife, refrigerate 1 hour before baking.
Bake at 220 C (425 F) about 15 minutes.

Plate Presentation

When the blanc-manger is set, unmold and place on the plate. Ladle raspberry coulis over a portion of the dome.
Cut the freshly baked pastry in two and fill with the warm fruits. Place on the plate and garnish with fresh red fruits and chocolate disks.

120

"Duguesclin"

"Duguesclin" is the name given to a light mixture of ground almonds and pastry cream. It is a delicious filling for desserts layered with cake. Vanilla crème anglaise and chocolate decorations complete this dessert.

Ingredients

Biscuit russe
Duguesclin cream
Powdered sugar

Decoration:
Chocolate disks
Chocolate curls

Sauce:
Vanilla crème anglaise

Procedure

Pipe the cake batter into 7 cm (3 in) circles on a baking sheet.
Bake at 200 C (400 F) for about 20 minutes.
Layer the cooled cakes with Duguesclin cream in the center then cover the desserts with a thin, smooth layer of cream
Place in the refrigerator for 1/2 hour.
Make the vanilla crème anglaise and the chocolate decorations.

Plate Presentation

Coat the chilled "Dugueslins" with powdered sugar.
Place them on the plate and ladle crème anglaise around the dessert.
Garnish with the chocolate disks.

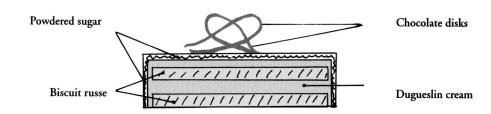

Powdered sugar

Chocolate disks

Biscuit russe

Dugueslin cream

121

Walnut Ice Cream with "Croustillants"

Lacy, crispy "croustillants" are made with walnuts to marry with the walnut ice cream. Caramel sauce and white chocolate decorations are an elegant finishing touch.

Ingredients

Walnut "croustillants"
Walnut ice cream

Decoration:
White chocolate disks

Sauce:
Caramel sauce

Procedure

Make the walnut croustillants and keep them crisp in an air tight container.
Make the white chocolate disks.
Make the walnut ice cream and caramel sauce.

Plate Presentation

Alternate three scoops of ice cream with three croustillants.
Spoon caramel sauce over half of each scoop of ice cream.
Decorate with the white chocolate disks.

Chapter 5 - Chocolate Desserts

Introduction **Chocolate**

The use of chocolate in fancy French desserts has evolved over the last few years with the distribution of a wider variety of products.
Here is some advise for choosing cocoa-based products:
Cocoa powder: For decoration, choose the darkest cocoa available but for flavoring cakes, etc., choose one with a more subtle flavor.
Covering chocolate: Bittersweet chocolate with 64% cocoa butter will melt well and give the best results.
White covering chocolate: Choose a white chocolate from a reputable company with a creamy color.
Baking chocolate: Choose a bittersweet chocolate with a strong flavor to blend into mousses, creams and ganaches.

1. Chocolate Leaves with Chocolate Mousse and Hazelnut Meringue
2. Chocolate "Pavé" with Coffee Créme Anglaise
3. Chocolate Mousse
4. "Profiteroles"
5. Chocolate Mousse with Grand Marnier Sabayon.
6. Chocolate and Pear "Bûche"

Chocolate Leaves with Mousse and Hazelnut Meringue

Hazelnuts and chocolate are delicious together, with a wonderful bittersweet flavor. This fancy dessert combines a hazelnut meringue, chocolate mousse, with thin chocolate disks and crème anglaise.

Ingredients

Hazelnut meringue
  ("dacquoise")
Chocolate mousse
Chocolate "leaves"

Decoration:
Powdered sugar
Cocoa powder
Two-toned cigarettes
Sauce:
Vanilla crème anglaise

Procedure

Pipe the meringue mixture in oval shapes on a baking sheet.
Cook at 200 C (400 F) about 15-20 minutes.
Cool then trim to a perfect oval using an oval cutter.
Use the same oval cutter, dipped in hot water (and wiped dry) to cut out oval disks of tempered covering chocolate.
Make the two-toned chocolate cigarettes, the chocolate mousse, and the vanilla crème anglaise.

Plate Presentation

Pipe chocolate mousse on a layer of meringue.
Cover with a chocolate "leaf", pipe on chocolate mousse and top with a chocolate leaf. (Choose the best ones for the top.)
Sprinkle the top with a little powdered sugar and arrange two desserts on each plate.
Spoon crème anglaise around and sprinkle with a little cocoa powder. Decorate with the two-toned chocolate cigarettes.

Chocolate leaves

Chocolate mousse

Hazelnut meringue

Chocolate "Pavé" with Coffee Crème Anglaise

This rich chocolate dessert combines layers of chocolate sponge cake and ganache with a coffee-flavored crème anglaise.

Ingredients

Chocolate sponge cake
Sugar syrup with chocolate
Ganache
Covering chocolate

Decoration:
Chocolate fans
Powdered sugar

Sauce:
Coffee crème anglaise

Procedure

Make two sheet of chocolate sponge cake 40 cm X 60 cm (16 in X 24 in). Cut the cooled cakes in half.
Spread a thin layer of tempered covering chocolate on one of the strips of cakes and cool to set. Turn it over and moisten with syrup.
Spread a layer (3 mm (1/8 in)) of ganache and cover with a strip of imbibed cake. Top with a smooth layer of ganache.
Place in the freezer about 1 hour to make the ganache firm.
Make the chocolate fans and coffee crème anglaise.

Plate Presentation

Decorate the top of the chilled pavé with tempered chocolate, drizzled with a spoon or sprayed from a patissier's "pistolet".
Cut individual portions about 7 cm X 4 cm (3 in X 1 1/2 in).
Place on the plate with coffee crème anglaise.
Decorate with powdered sugar and chocolate fans.

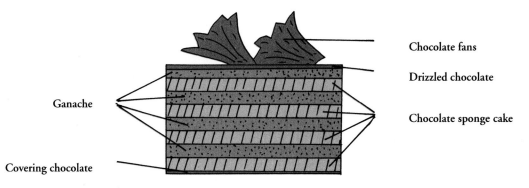

Chocolate fans

Drizzled chocolate

Chocolate sponge cake

Ganache

Covering chocolate

Chocolate Mousse

This favorite child's dessert is presented elegantly with buttery orange Florentine cookies and two-toned chocolate cigarettes. All the elements can be made ahead for easy service in a restaurant or at home

Ingredients

Chocolate mousse

Decoration:
Orange florentines
Two-toned chocolate cigarettes.

Procedure

Make the florentines and chocolate cigarettes.
Make the chocolate mousse.

Plate Presentation

Spoon a dollop of mousse into a beautiful goblet or bowl.
Decorate with the florentines and chocolate cigarettes.

"Profiteroles"

A popular dessert in French restaurants, profiteroles are small cream puffs filled with vanilla ice cream, piled on the plate and served with warm chocolate sauce. The filled puffs can be kept frozen and the chocolate sauce can stay warm in a water bath for easy assembly.

Ingredients

Small cream puffs
Vanilla ice cream

Sauce:
Chocolate sauce

Procedure

Pipe small mounds of choux pastry on a heavy baking sheet and bake at 220 C (425 F) about 20 minutes or until puffed and golden brown. Place on a rack to cool.
With a serrated knife, make a slice to form a cap with a "hinge".
Make the vanilla ice cream and fill each cream puff with a scoop.
Arrange the filled puffs in a single layer on a tray in the freezer.
Make the chocolate sauce and keep warm in a water bath.

Plate Presentation

Make a small mound of the profiteroles and at the last moment, ladle warm chocolate sauce over the top of the puffs.

Chocolate Mousse with Grand Marnier Sabayon

Almond meringue forms a crispy base for layers of chocolate mousse and almond sponge cake. Grand Marnier flavors the sabayon sauce and the imbibing syrup for the cake.

Ingredients

Almond meringue ("succès")
Almond sponge cake
Sugar syrup with Grand Marnier
Chocolate mousse
Chocolate glaze

Decoration:
Chocolate truffles
Mint leaves
Chocolate rectangles

Sauce:
Grand Marnier sabayon

Procedure

Place a circle of almond meringue in the base of a high-sided pastry ring. Pipe a layer of chocolate mousse on top.
Place a circle of almond sponge cake moistened with sugar syrup then fill the mold to the top with mousse.
Place in the freezer about 2 hours to become firm.
Make the chocolate glaze, chocolate rectangles, truffles and the Grand Marnier sabayon.

Plate Presentation

Coat the top of the chilled dessert with chocolate glaze.
When the glaze has set, remove the rings and place in the center of the plate.
Press the chocolate rectangles in an overlapping pattern around the mousse. Decorate with a truffle and a mint leaf.
Spoon the Grand Marnier sabayon around the dessert.

Chocolate truffle

Chocolate glaze

Chocolate mousse

Mint leaf

Almond sponge cake with Grand Marnier syrup

Almond meringue

Chocolate and Pear "Bûche"

A delicious combination of chocolate sponge cake, poached pears and hazelnut meringue makes this traditional Christmas dessert special.

Ingredients

Hazelnut meringue
  ("dacquoise")
Chocolate sponge cake
Chocolate mousse
Pear-flavored sugar syrup
Poached pears
Chocolate glaze

Decoration:
Chocolate fans
Tiny pears, poached
Chocolate truffles

Sauce:
Vanilla crème anglaise

Procedure

Line a cylindrical mold with plastic wrap then with a layer of chocolate sponge cake moistened with sugar syrup.
Fill halfway with chocolate mousse, arrange poached pear slices over the mousse then fill almost to the top with mousse.
Cover the mousse with a rectangle of hazelnut meringue and place in the freezer to firm about 2 hours.
Unmold the chilled "bûche" and coat with chocolate glaze.
Cut a thin slice from each end for a neat appearance.
The entire cake can be garnished or add decorations to the individual servings.

Plate Presentation

Cut the cake into 2.5 cm (1 in) slices and place two slices on the plate.
Pour vanilla crème anglaise around the slices.
Decorate with chocolate fans, truffles and the tiny pear which can be brushed with coffee syrup to make it golden.

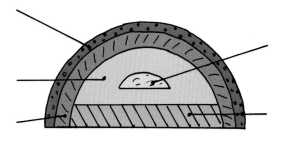

Chocolate glaze

Pear slices

Chocolate mousse

Chocolate sponge cake
with pear syrup

Hazelnut meringue

Introduction   **Coffee**

A dessert made with coffee should have a pretty color, a strong aroma and not be too sweet. In France, a concentrated coffee syrup is available to flavor pastries. Top quality instant coffees, diluted double strength or freshly ground, brewed double strength espresso will give good results.

1. **Coffee Charlotte with Apricot Coulis**
2. **"Moka"**
3. **Nougatine "Succès"**
4. **"Equator"**
5. **Rum Raisin and Coffee "Bombe"**

Coffee Charlotte with Apricot Coulis

In France this dessert carries the name "Charlotte Brésilienne" because good coffee comes from Brazil. Caramelized apricots and an apricot mousse and coulis adds an interesting counterpoint to the coffee bavarian cream.

Ingredients
Ladyfingers with cocoa
Chocolate sponge cake
Sugar syrup with coffee
Apricot mousse
Coffee bavarian cream
Coffee-flavored jelly glaze

Decoration:
Caramelized apricot halves
White chocolate disks
Chocolate coffee beans

Sauces:
Apricot coulis

Procedure
Place a strip of ladyfingers, dusted with cocoa powder, (cut to go up about 2/3 the way up the mold) around the sides of the mold.

Place a layer of chocolate sponge cake moistened with syrup in the bottom. Fill halfway with apricot mousse and place in the freezer about 30 minutes or until firm. Fill with coffee bavarian and smooth the top. Place in the freezer about 2 hours to set.

Caramelize the apricot halves and make the white chocolate disks. Make the apricot coulis and the coffee crème anglaise.

Plate Presentation
Coat the top of the mold with the jelly glaze flavored with coffee. Remove the mold and place on the plate.

Decorate the plate with the two sauces piped out with a paper cone. Decorate with the caramelized apricots, chocolate coffee beans and the white chocolate disks.

White chocolate disks

Coffee glaze

Ladyfingers with cocoa

Caramelized apricot halves

Coffee bavarian

Apricot mousse

Chocolate sponge cake with coffee syrup

"Moka"

Moka can be found in pastry shops throughout France. Here it is made fancy for an elegant plate presentation.

Ingredients

Genoise
Coffee-flavored sugar syrup
Coffee buttercream

Sauce:
Vanilla crème anglaise

Decoration:
Chopped almonds, toasted
Two-toned cigarettes
Chocolate disks
Coffee syrup

Procedure

Place a cicle of genoise, moistened with coffee-flavored syrup in the bottom of a high-sided pastry ring.
Pipe a layer of coffee buttercream on the cake.
Cover with another layer of imbibed cake and fill with buttercream and smooth the top.
Place in the freezer about 30 minutes to become firm.
Toast the chopped almonds, make the chocolate disks and cigarettes, and coffee crème anglaise.

Plate Presentation

Remove the rings from the chilled desserts.
Spread coffee buttercream around the sides and press the toasted almonds 2/3 the way up the sides.
Place on the plate and decorate the top with buttercream piped in a pretty design, add the chocolate disks and cigarette.
Pour coffee crème anglaise on the plate and add a few drops of coffee syrup and swirl for a marbled effect.

Two-toned cigarette

Chocolate disk

Coffee buttercream

Genoise with coffee syrup

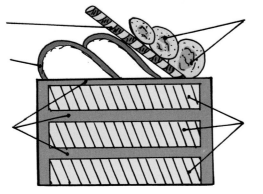

Nougatine "Succès"

Similar to the classic dessert "Succès" of baked nut meringues with layers of buttercream, this version adds a crunchy circle of nougatine and is served with a coffee crème anglaise.

Ingredients

Coffee buttercream
Almond meringue ("succès")
Almond brittle ("nougatine")

Sauce:
Coffee crème anglaise

Decoration:
Two-toned cigarettes
Chocolate decorations
Marbled chocolate disks

Procedure

Pipe out circles of almond meringue and bake (2 per serving).
Trim the baked meringues to the same size with a round cutter.
Cut disks the same size (one per serving) from nougatine.
Pipe buttercream on one circle of meringue, cover with another and press to distribute the buttercream to the edges.
Pipe buttercream on top, place a nougatine disk and press gently.
Make the coffee crème anglaise, the chocolate disks, cigarettes, and decorations.

Plate Presentation

Place the dessert in the center, ladle the sauce on the side and arrange the chocolate decorations around the dessert.

Two toned cigarette

Chocolate decoration

Coffee buttercream

Marbled chocolate disk

Nougatine disk

Almond meringue

Equator

This dessert made with coffee buttercream salutes the countries that border the equator where delicious coffees are grown.

Ingredients

Biscuit russe	*Decoration:*
Coffee buttercream	Chocolate shavings
Covering chocolate	Powdered sugar
Chocolate glaze	Chocolate disks

Sauce:
Coffee crème anglaise

Procedure

Bake a sheet of "biscuit russe" and cool.
Cut the sheet in three and spread tempered covering chocolate over one strip of cake.
Turn the strip over and cover with coffee buttercream.
Continue layering cake and buttercream to achieve 5 layers.
Place in the freezer about 1 hour to become firm. Make the chocolate glaze, chocolate shavings and the coffee crème anglaise.

Plate Presentation

Coat the chilled cake with chocolate glaze. Chill to set.
Cut rectangles 7 cm x 5 cm (3 in x 2 in) and press a few chocolate shavings on one side.
Dust with a little powdered sugar and place on the plate.
Garnish with chocolates and ladle coffee crème anglaise on the plate.

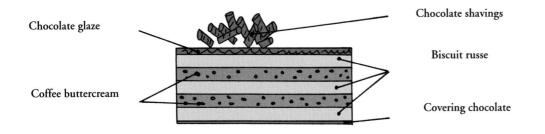

Chocolate glaze

Coffee buttercream

Chocolate shavings

Biscuit russe

Covering chocolate

Rum Raisin and Coffee Bombe

This frozen "bombe" consists of a rum raisin "parfait" and coffee ice cream and is served with a rum sabayon and chocolate fans.

Ingredients

Coffee ice cream
"Creole" (rum raisin) "parfait"
Almond sponge cake
Rum-flavored sugar syrup
Jelly glaze
Coffee syrup

Decoration:
Rum-macerated raisins
Chocolate fans

Sauce:
Rum sabayon

Procedure

Spread a layer of coffee ice cream on the inside of a dome shaped mold. Place in the freezer to firm this layer then fill the mold with rum raisin parfait. Moisten a circle of sponge cake with rum syrup and invert to cover the parfait. Place in the freezer several hours.

Make the chocolate fans and rum sabayon.

Plate Presentation

Unmold the domes and return to the freezer to thoroughly chill the surface before adding the jelly glaze.

Carefully swirl a little coffee syrup into the jelly glaze for a marbling effect and coat the frozen dome.

Place the dessert on the plate and place four chocolate fans around the dome then ladle rum sabayon around and add rum-macerated raisins.

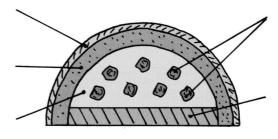

Marbled jelly glaze

Coffee ice cream

Rum raisin parfait

Rum-macerated raisins

Almond sponge cake with rum syrup

Introduction
Caramel and Tea

Cooking caramel to flavor a dessert is a delicate operation: too light and the flavor and color are "flat", too dark and the color is unattractive and the flavor is bitter.
The best tea to use in pastries is a Chinese tea that is not "smoky". It is better to infuse several bags for a shorter time than a small amount for a longer time–; lengthy infusing brings out a bitter taste.

1. "Crème Caramel" with Orange Sauce

2. Pear and Caramel Charlotte

3. Caramel Tart

4. Dessert for "Gourmands"

5. "Five O'Clock"

Crème Caramel with Orange Sauce

A simple bistrot dessert is improved with a tasty orange sauce and crispy cookies flavored with orange peel.

Ingredients

Caramel
Crème caramel mixture
Orange "croustillants"

Decoration:
Chocolate disks disks

Sauce:
Orange caramel sauce

Procedure

To make the caramel, cook 500 g (1 lb) sugar with 150 ml (5 fl oz) water until it becomes golden. Pour into the individual soufflé dishes and swirl to coat the sides.
Make the crème caramel mixture and fill the coated molds.
Cook in a water bath at 180 (350 F) about 35 minutes or until set.
Make the orange "croustillants" and store in an air tight container.
Make the chocolate disks and the orange caramel sauce.

Plate Presentation

Run a knife around the edge of the mold and invert the cooled crème caramel onto a plate.
Press the chocolate decorations around the edge.
Serve with the orange caramel sauce and the cookies.

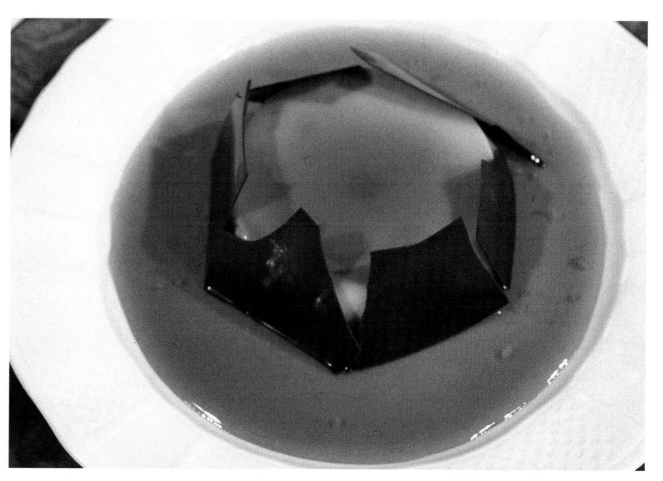

Pear and Caramel Charlotte

This delicious dessert combines the compatable flavors of pears and caramel with elegant decorations made from nougatine and chocolate.

Ingredients

Pear mousse
Caramel bavarian
Nougatine, crumbled
Ladyfingers with cocoa powder
Almond sponge cake
Coffee-flavored sugar syrup
Jelly glaze
Coffee syrup

Decoration:
Two-toned chocolate cigarettes
Chocolate disks
Poached pear slices
Rectangles of nougatine

Sauce:
Caramel sauce

Procedure

Fit a band of ladyfingers (cut to 2/3 the height of the mold and dusted with cocoa) inside high-sided pastry rings.
In the bottom, place a circle of almond sponge cake moistened with syrup. Fill halfway with pear mousse and place in the freezer about 30 minutes to set. Fill to the top with caramel bavarian with crushed nougatine added.
Return to the freezer about 2 hours or until thoroughly set.
Make the nougatine rectangles, the chocolate disks, slices of poached pears, two-toned cigarettes and the caramel sauce.

Plate Presentation

Coat the top of the chilled charlottes with jelly glaze swirled with coffee syrup. Unmold and place on the plate.
Decorate the top with a chocolate disk and cigarette.
Arrange three rectangles of nougatine and three pear slices on the plate and add the caramel sauce.

Swirled jelly glaze

Crumbled nougatine

Ladyfingers with cocoa

Pear mousse

Chocolate disk

Two-toned cigarette

Caramel bavarian

Almond sponge cake
with coffee syrup

Caramel Ice Cream Tart

Crunchy nougatine holds a scoop of creamy caramel ice cream. The tart is decorated with caramelized nuts and served with two sauces.

Ingredients

Nougatine
Caramel ice cream
Caramelized nuts

Sauces
Vanilla crème anglaise
Caramel sauce

Procedure

Cut out disks of nougatine. Mold circles of warm nougatine into tart molds.
With a little hot caramel, «glue» the molded nougatines to the disks.
Make the caramel ice cream, caramelized nuts, vanilla crème anglaise, and caramel sauce.

Plate Presentation

Spoon a little caramel sauce in the bottom of each molded nougatine.
Place a scoop of ice cream in the «bowl» and garnish with nuts.
Serve with vanilla crème anglaise.

Caramel ice cream

Caramel nuts

Nougatine

Sauce caramel

Dessert for "Gourmands"

For gourmets with a hearty appetite, here are three desserts: a tea bavarian, a lemon tart, and chocolate mousse served together in a spectacular display.

Ingredients

Almond sponge cake (striped)
Lemon-flavored sugar syrup
Tea bavarian cream
Sweet pie pastry
Lemon filling
Chocolate mousse
Jelly glaze

Decorations:

Candied citrus peel
Powdered sugar
Raspberries
Mint leaves
Chocolate disks

Sauce:
Tea flavored caramel sauce

Procedure

Tea bavarian: Place a strip of almond sponge cake around a high-sided pastry ring.
Place a circle of cake, moistened with lemon-flavored syrup, in the bottom.
Fill with tea bavarian and place in the freezer to set.
Lemon tart: Line tart molds with sweet pie pastry. Fill with lemon filling. Bake at 220 C (425 F) about 15 minutes. Remove molds and cool.
Chocolate mousse with chocolate leaves: Pipe chocolate mousse between three chocolate disks. Refrigerate until service.

Plate Presentation

Coat the top of the tea bavarian and the lemon tart with melted jelly glaze.
Sprinkle powdered sugar over the chocolate dessert. Ladle tea caramel sauce on the plate and arrange the three desserts.
Decorate with candied citrus peel, raspberries and mint leaves.

Raspberry	Mint leaf
Jelly glaze	Tea bavarian
Almond sponge cake with lemon syrup	Striped almond sponge cake
	Candied citrus peel
Sweet pie pastry	Lemon curd

Five O'Clock

Perfect with a cup of tea at five o'clock, this refined dessert combines lemon sponge cake and frozen tea mousse presented on a thin nougatine. Oval, high-sided pastry rings are used for this presentation but another shape could be used.

Ingredients

Frozen tea mousse
Almond sponge cake
Lemon-flavored sugar syrup
Crushed nougatine

Decoration:
Nougatine disks
Chocolate disks
Two-toned chocolate cigarettes

Sauce:
Tea caramel sauce

Procedure

Place a layer of almond sponge cake in the bottom of each mold, moisten with lemon-flavored syrup and fill with tea mousse.
Place in the freezer for 2 hours to set.
Make the nougatine and chocolate disks and the tea-infused caramel sauce. Use "scraps" from forming the disks to make the finely crumbled nougatine.

Plate Presentation

When the mousse is frozen, cover the top with crumbled nougatine and remove the mold.
Place the mousse on a disk of nougatine in the center of the plate and press the chocolate disks around the egde.
Add the caramel sauce and garnish with chocolate cigarettes.

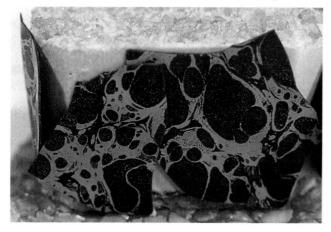

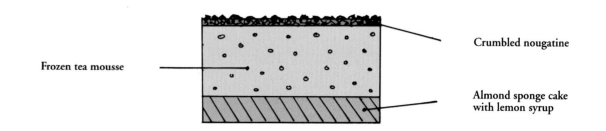

Crumbled nougatine

Frozen tea mousse

Almond sponge cake
with lemon syrup

Introduction
Vanilla and Praline

Choose moist vanilla beans with a good aroma to give the best flavor to desserts where the vanilla taste is the "star". Pure vanilla extract can be used but imitation products will not give good results.
Praline is a paste of toasted nuts and caramel that gives an intense flavor to pastries. It is available from pastry suppliers. In France praline is made with with just almonds (light or strong flavor) and with hazelnuts and almonds mixed.

1. Hazelnut "Sablée" with Vanilla Cream

2. Vacherin with Raspberry Coulis

3. Floating Island with "Cassis" Caramel

4. Almond "Succés"

5. Praline Dome with Rum Sabayon

6. Praline Cream Puffs

Hazelnut "Sablés" with Vanilla Cream

Melt-in-your-mouth hazelnut cookies or "sablés" are sandwiched with light vanilla pastry cream and served with mango coulis.

Ingredients

Hazelnut sablé dough
Light vanilla cream
Chocolate disks

Sauce:
Mango coulis

Decorations:
Toasted hazelnuts
Vanilla beans

Procedure

Roll out the pastry dough very thin and cut out circles of several different sizes. Bake at 220 C (425 F) a few minutes until golden and transfer to a cooling rack.

Cut out circles of tempered covering chocolate the same sizes as the cookies (there should be two of each size cookie and one of chocolate for each serving). Peel and toast the hazelnuts, make the light vanilla cream and make the mango coulis.

Plate Presentation

Match up the various sizes of circles and make stacks of two cookies with a chocolate disk on top with cream between the layers. Spoon mango coulis on the plate, arrange the stacks of cookies, cream and chocolate around and decorate with a vanilla bean and toasted hazelnuts.

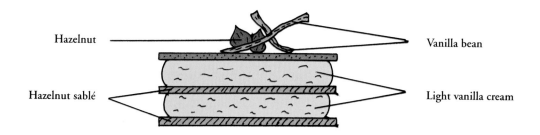

Hazelnut — Vanilla bean

Hazelnut sablé — Light vanilla cream

Vacherin and Raspberry Coulis

The classic dessert "Vacherin" is a crispy meringue filled with ice cream. This individual presentation has a colorful garnish of red fruits and the tart raspberry sauce is the ideal counterpoint to the sweet meringue.

Ingredients

Vanilla ice cream
French meringue
Genoise
Raspberry-flavored sugar syrup
Whipped cream

Decoration:
Sliced almonds
Red fruits
Vanilla bean
Sauce:
Raspberry coulis

Procedure

Pipe out circles (6 cm (about 2 1/2 in)) of French meringue and bake at 100 C (200 F) about 2 hours. Transfer to a cooling rack. Cut circles of cake the same size as the meringues and moisten with raspberry-flavored syrup. Place a scoop of homemade vanilla ice cream on one circle of meringue. Cover with a circle of imbibed cake, another layer of ice cream then top with a circle of meringue. Cover and store in the freezer.
Toast the sliced almonds, make the raspberry sauce ("coulis"), prepare the red fruits and whip the cream to soft peaks.

Plate Presentation

Spread whipped cream over the entire surface of the frozen vacherin. Press toasted almonds 2/3 the way up the sides.
Pipe more whipped cream in a decorative design with a little well on top and fill with red fruits and bits of vanilla bean.
Serve with raspberry coulis.

Red fruits

Vanilla ice cream

Whipped cream

Sponge cake
wich raspberry syrup

French meringue

Floating Island with Black Currant Caramel Sauce

Floating Island or "Ile Flottant" can be a simple poached meringue drizzled with caramel swimming in a pool of crème anglaise or it can be taken to new heights as in this dessert with caramel flavored with black currant liqueur (crème de cassis") and a decorative sugar cage.

Ingredients

Meringue (poached)

Decoration:
Cooked sugar cage

Sauces:
Caramel sauce with cassis
Vanilla crème anglaise

Procedure

To make the meringue, whip 250 ml (1 cup) egg whites to soft peaks. Whisk in 200 g (6 1/2 oz or 1 cup) until the meringue is firm, smooth and glossy.
Form "quenelles" (football-shaped scoops) of meringue with two soup spoons and drop them gently into simmering milk to poach for 2 minutes. Transfer to a dish towel to drain.
Use the milk from poaching the meringues to make the crème anglaise. Pour through a sieve and chill.
Make the caramel sauce with cassis.
Make the sugar cages to fit the top of the serving bowls.

Plate Presentation

Fill a bowl about 2/3 with crème anglaise.
Place three meringues on the sauce and drizzle the cassis caramel sauce over the meringues.
Cover the bowl with the sugar cage.

Almond "Succès"

"Succès" is one of the most "successful" of the classic French desserts. A slice of this crunchy meringue with rich buttercream is served here with coffee crème anglaise.

Ingredients

Almond "succès"
Meringue
Praline buttercream

Sauce:
Coffee crème anglaise

Decoration:
Toasted sliced almonds
Chocolate shavings

Procedure

Pipe out two circles (20 cm (8 in)) of almond meringue ("succès") and one circle of plain meringue and bake until crispy.
Make the praline buttercream.
Toast the slices almonds.
Spread one layer of almond meringue with buttercream.
Cover with the circle of plain meringue, spread with buttercream then cover with the second layer of almond meringue.
Spread buttercream around the sides and press the toasted sliced almonds on the sides. Chill if necessary for easy slicing.

Plate Presentation

Sprinkle the top of the cake with powdered sugar.
Cut into servings and place one on a plate accompanied by the crème anglaise.
Decorate with the chocolate shavings.

Toasted sliced almonds

Plain meringue

Almond meringue

Praline buttercream

Praline Dome
with Rum Sabayon

Praline ice cream, formed in a dome-shaped mold with a layer of rum "parfait", is presented on a disk of almond brittle.

Ingredients

Praline ice cream
Rum "parfait"
Chocolate sponge cake
Sugar syrup with rum
Jelly glaze

Decoration:
Nougatine disks
Chocolate curls
Chocolate twigs

Sauce:
Rum sabayon

Procedure

Spread a thin layer of praline ice cream on the inside of a dome-shaped molds. Place in the freezer to harden.
Fill the center with rum "parfait" and on the top place a circle of chocolate sponge cake moistened with rum syrup.
Place in the freezer for several hours.
Unmold and reserve in the freezer.
Make the nougatine disks (slightly larger than the diameter of the domes).
Make the chocolate twigs and curls. Make the rum sabayon.

Plate Presentation

Brush jelly glaze (melted and cooled) on the frozen dome.
Place the dome on a nougatine disk and place on the plate.
Spoon rum sabayon around the dessert and decorate with with chocolate twigs and curls.

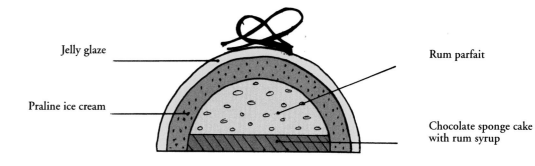

Jelly glaze

Praline ice cream

Rum parfait

Chocolate sponge cake with rum syrup

Praline Cream Puffs

The shape of these cream puffs are known as "Salambos" and here are filled with praline pastry cream and whipped cream and served with crème anglaise.

Ingredients

Cream puff dough
  (pâte à choux)
Praline cream mousseline
Whipped cream
Cooked sugar (caramel)

Decoration:
Chocolate decorations

Sauce:
Crème anglaise
(with cocoa powder)

Procedure

Make the praline cream and whipped cream.
Pipe out small, thick "eclairs" or "salambos" and bake until puffed and golden.
Coat the top of the puffs with sugar cooked to a light caramel.
Cut one side of the "salambos" with a serrated knife, open enough to pipe in the praline cream and whipped cream.
Press gently to close the top a little without disturbing the cream inside.
Make the crème anglaise and chocolate decorations.

Plate Presentation

Place two salambos on the plate, spoon crème anglaise around and sprinkle with cocoa powder.
Garnish with the chocolate decorations.

Cooked sugar (caramel) —
Cream puff —
— Whipped cream
— Praline cream

150

Introduction
"Fromage Blanc", Mint, Licorice, Coconut

French "fromage blanc" is a fresh cheese similar to ricotta. For best results, drain ricotta in a coffee filter about 1 hour before using. To augment mint flavor in desserts, a drop of mint oil or extract can be added to a mint-infused infused liquid. Licorice powder and extract together deliver a well-rounded licorice flavor. Check specialty pastry suppliers for these products.

Frozen coconut is now available which eliminates the tedious task of splitting and scraping out the flesh of fresh coconuts. Canned or flaked coconut in bags does not give enough flavor to these desserts.

1. Fresh Cheese Mousse with Nougatine
2. Fresh Cheese Mousse with Red Fruits and Chocolate
3. Mint "Pavé"
4. Mint Granité in a Chocolate Cup
5. Chocolate Licorice Tart
6. Frozen Licorice Parfait
7. "Bermuda Triangle"
8. "Souvenir from the Islands"

Fresh Cheese Mousse with Nougatine and Chocolate

"Fromage blanc" is a fresh cheese similar to ricotta. This mousse is like an extra-light cheesecake and is delicious with chopped nougatine and thin disks of chocolate.

Ingredients

"Fromage blanc" mousse
Nougatine, chopped
Striped chocolate case
Jelly glaze

Decoration:
Red currants

Sauce:
Red currant coulis

Procedure

Make the striped tear-shaped chocolate case.
Stir chopped nougatine into the fresh cheese mousse.
Pipe the mousse between layers of the chocolate and chill in the freezer for about 1 hour.
Make the red currant coulis.

Plate Presentation

Brush jelly glaze on the mousse.
Ladle red currant coulis on the plate and place the dessert in the center.
Decorate the top with a small bunch of red currants.

Jelly glaze

Striped chocolate disk

Fresh cheese mousse

Red currants

Chopped nougatine

Fresh Cheese Mousse with Fruits

A delicate version of a cheesecake, this fresh cheese mousse is topped with an assortment of red fruits and served with a raspberry coulis.

Ingredients

Alomnd sponge cake, striped
Fresh cheese mousse
Vanilla-flavored sugar syrup

Sauce:
Raspberry coulis

Decoration:
Whipped cream
Red fruits

Procedure

Cut a strip of sponge cake to line the inside (2/3 the way up) of a high-sided pastry ring. Place a circle of cake in the bottom and moisten with syrup. Fill with fresh cheese mousse and smooth the top with a metal spatula.
Place in the freezer about 2 hours to set. Prepare the red fruits, make the raspberry coulis and whipped cream.

Plate Presentation

Remove the ring from the chilled dessert and place on the plate.
Pipe whipped cream in a decorative design and garnish with red fruits. Spoon the raspberry coulis around the mouuse.

Whipped cream

Fresh cheese mousse

Sponge cake with vanilla syrup

Red fruits

Striped sponge cake

Mint "Pavé"

A refreshing dessert that combines a mint bavarian with chocolate sponge cake and chocolate decorations. If rectangular individual molds are not available, it can be assembled in a long mold and cut into portions.

Ingredients

Mint bavarian cream
Chocolate sponge cake
Mint-flavored sugar syrup
Jelly glaze (with green color)

Decoration:
Chocolate decoartions
Red currants
Mint leaves
Chocolate glaze

Procedure

Place a layer of chocolate sponge cake in the bottom of the mold and moisten wth syrup.
Fill with mint bavarian, smooth the top and place in the freezer about 2 hours or until set.
Make the chocolate decorations.

Plate Presentation

Coat the top with jelly glaze that has been tinted green and flavored with mint.
Remove the mold and place on the plate. Pipe chocolate glaze and green jelly glaze on the plate in a decorative design.
Place the chocolate decorations on the sides and garnish the top with a little bunch of red currants and mint leaves.

Red currants

Jelly glaze

Mint leaves

Mint bavarian

Chocolate sponge cake
with mint syrup

154

Mint Granité in a Chocolate Cup

Refreshing mint granité served in an elegant chocolate cup with chocolate mousse.

Ingredients

Chocolate cup
Chocolate mousse
Mint granité

Decoration:
Red fruits
Mint leaves

Sauce:
Red fruit coulis

Procedure

Mold covering chocolate over a demi-sphere to form a cup.
Make a disk of chocolate to make the "saucer".
Fill the cup with chocolate mousse and place in the freezer about 30 minutes to set.
Make the mint granité and the red fruit coulis.

Plate Presentation

Decorate the chocolate cup with drizzled chocolate (or use a pastry "pistol").
Scoop the mint granité and place on top of the mousse.
Garnish with fruits and a mint leaf and serve with red fruit coulis.

Mint leaves

Mint granité

Chocolate mousse

Chocolate decor

Covering chocolate cup

Chocolate Licorice Tart

Natural licorice sticks, a favorite treat for French children, can still be found in French markets. The ganache that fills this tart is flavored with natural licorice powder which can be found through specialty food mail order.

Ingredients

Hazelnut sablé pastry
Chocolate sponge cake
Licorice-flavored sugar syrup
Licorice ganache

Decoration:
Two-toned chocolate cigarettes
Chocolate disks

Sauce:
Vanilla créme anglaise

Procedure

Press circles of pastry into 7 cm (3 in) pastry rings. Prick with a fork and bake at 200 C (400 F) for 8-10 minutes.
Remove the rings, trim the baked pastries and cool.
Place a rond of chocolate sponge cake, moistened with syrup, in the bottom of the tart shell then pipe licorice ganache to the top. Refrigerate for 2 hours to become firm.
Make the crème anglaise, two-toned cigarettes and the chocolate disks.

Plate Presentation

Cover the bottom of the plate with crème anglaise and place the tart in the center.
Decorate with a chocolate cigarette and disk.

Two-toned cigarette

Licorice ganache

Chocolate sponge cake
with licorice syrup

Chocolate disk

Hazelnut pastry

156

Frozen Licorice "Parfait"

Licorice flavors a frozen "parfait" mixture which is served on a nougatine disk and decorated with chocolate. If a hexagonal mold is not available, use a high-sided ring mold.

Ingredients

Licorice "parfait" mixture
Almond sponge cake
Licorice-flavored sugar syrup
Chocolate glaze

Sauce:
Vanilla crème anglaise
  with coffee syrup

Decoration:
Nougatine
Chocolate disks
Chocolate curls

Procedure

Place a layer of almond sponge cake in the bottom of the molds and moisten with syrup.
Fill with licorice parfait and smooth the top.
Place in the freezer for to hours.
Make the nougatine disks, chocolate disks, the chocolate curls, the vanilla crème anglaise and the chocolate glaze.

Plate Presentation

Coat the frozen parfait with chocolate glaze.
Remove the mold and place on a nougatine disk.
Place on the plate and spoon crème anglaise around.
Add a few drops of coffee syrup and swirl for a marbled effect.
Decorate with the chocolate disks and curls.

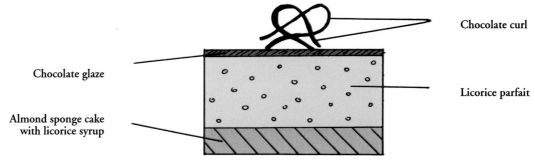

Chocolate curl

Chocolate glaze

Licorice parfait

Almond sponge cake
with licorice syrup

Bermuda Triangle

Triangles of coconut mousse and coconut meringue with red currant mousse and tropical fruits are served with a coconut sauce.

Ingredients

Coconut meringue	*Decoration:*
Coconut mousse	Tropical fruits, red currants
Red currant mousse	Chocolate disks
Covering chocolate	Jelly glaze

Sauce:
Coconut sauce

Procedure

Spread tempered covering chocolate on a layer of coconut meringue and invert it into the bottom of a rectangular mold.
Fill halfway with red currant mousse and chill in the freezer about 30 minutes.
Fill with coconut mousse and smooth the top.
Place in the freezer about 2 hours or until set.
Make the coconut sauce.
Prepare the fruits and make the chocolate disks.

Plate Presentation

Coat the top of the mousse with jelly glaze.
Cut into triangles, decorate with red currants, and place on the plate with the fruits, chocolate disks and coconut sauce.

Jelly glaze — Red currants

Red currant mousse — Coconut mousse

Covering chocolate — Coconut meringue

Souvenir from the Islands

A dessert straight from an island paradise, a chocolate coconut shell filled with coconut sorbet, served with passion fruit sauce and tropical fruits.

Ingredients

Coconut sorbet
Chocolate cup
Shredded coconut

Sauce:
Passion fruit sauce

Decoration:
Tropical fruits

Procedure

Make half spheres from covering chocolate.
Unmold and fill with coconut sorbet. Make a hollow in the center of the sorbet to make it look like a split coconut.
Place in the freezer for 30 minutes.
Prepare the tropical fruits and make the passion fruit sauce.

Plate Presentation

Sprinkle the shredded coconut over the top and place on the plate.
Decorate with the tropical fruits and serve with the passion fruit sauce.

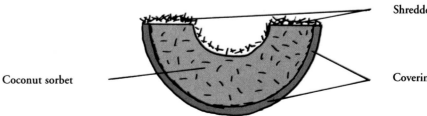

Shredded coconut

Coconut sorbet

Covering chocolate

159

Chapter 6 - Information and Technical Advice

- ## Recommendations and advice
  (for each recipe)

  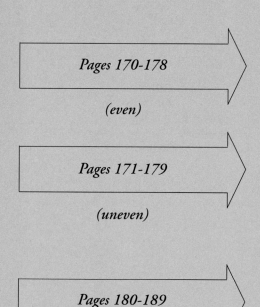

  Pages 162 à 169

- ## Information charts
  - A - Decoration, techniques
    and ingredients

    Pages 170-178

    (even)

  - B - Decorations, degree of difficulty,
    basic recipes

    Pages 171-179

    (uneven)

- ## Basic recipes of French patisserie

  Pages 180-189

- ## Equipment, additional information

  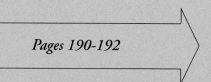

  Pages 190-192

Fresh Summer Fruits

1. Fresh Fruit Charlotte (page 38)

Presentation
Arrange the fruits in a decorative yet natural pattern. Juxtapose colors that compliment each other and make the most of the shapes to give height and volume.

Technique
Brush a light coat of jelly glaze on the fruits to make them shine.

Ingredients
The combination of fruit in the charlotte and the coulis can be changed with the season.

2. Harlequin Tart (page 39)

Presentation
Same advice as for the Fresh Fruit Charlotte.

Technique
Moisten the cake thoroughly with syrup and coat the fruits lightly with glaze.

Ingredients
Any combinaton of seasonal fruits can be used.

3. "Croustillants" (page 40)

Presentation
Arrange the fruits on the cream, alternating the colors, and place the croustillants on top so that the fruits show through and can be seen around the edge.

Technique
Arrange the ingredients on the plate just before serving with a chilled, firm cream and crispy cookies that have been stored in an air-tight container.

Ingredients
The light pastry cream can be replaced by whipped cream, and a fruit coulis can replace the caramel sauce.

4. Fresh Fruits in Crispy Pastry (page 41)

Presentation
Fold the filo dough so that the fruits can be seen through the thin pastry. Use the same fruits to garnish the plate.

Technique
Thoroughly cook the almond cream and fruits. Serve warm.

Ingredients
The filo can be shaped like a "beggar's purse".

5. Warm Apricot Tart (page 42)

Presentation
Sprinkle the tops of the apricots with sugar, then caramelize by using a torch or setting the apricots under the broiler.

Technique
Cook the pastry shells thoroughly and serve warm.

Ingredients
The pastry can be shaped in different form, and the tart can be served with a crème anglaise.

6. Peach and Almond Delight (page 43)

Presentation
Make the same design on the dessert and on the plate. Separate the apricot slices to fill the plate without using too much fruit per serving. Swirl a few drops of cassis into the caramel for a marbled effect.

Technique
Sprinkle very lightly and evenly with cocoa powder before glazing.

Ingredients
The mousse can be made with another fruit. Be sure to marry the flavor of the syrup and the garnish with the mousse.

Red Fruits

1. Raspberry "Croustillants" with Red Fruits (page 45)

Presentation
Place the cookies around the edge of one half of the plate in an attractive pattern, following the contour of the plate.

Technique
Glaze the strawberries before placing them on the plate. Use cream that is lightly whipped to soft peaks.

Ingredients
The whipped cream can be replaced by light, vanilla pasty cream.

2. Raspberry Dome (page 46)

Presentation
Place the dome in the exact center of the plate and arrange the berries in a neat circle around the edge of the pastry. The sabayon sauce should cover the bottom of the plate.

Technique
The dome must be very firm and chilled before coating with glaze.

Ingredients
Another fruit can be used to make the dome. Use the same fruit for the garnish and the sauce.

3. Red Fruit Tart (page 47)

Presentation
Same advice as for the Fresh Fruit Charlotte. The crème anglaise should cover the bottom of the plates.

Technique advice
Coat the fruits lightly with glaze.

Ingredients
The tart can be served without a sauce.

4. Blackberry "Pavé" (page 48)

Presentation
The various layers of the pavé are the "decoration" for this dessert. Carefully slice as soon as the dessert comes out of the freezer; use a sharp, thin knife dipped in hot water to make neat slices. Use just a little caramel sauce, and few drops of coulis is enough.

Technique
Use a spatula to spread the jelly glaze on the top of the pavé.

Ingredients
The mousse in the pavé can be made with any fruit.

5. Napoleon with Strawberries (page 49)

Presentation
Carefully garnish the three dollops of whipped cream with strawberry halves that have been glazed with melted jelly. Don't use too much sauce.

Technique
Bake the pastry layers thoroughly.

Ingredients
The strawberries can be replaced with another fresh red fruit.

Black Currant ("Cassis") Desserts

1. Almond Tart with Black Currants (page 51)

Presentation
To thoroughly coat the black currants with jelly glaze, pour melted glaze in a bowl add the "cassis", stir to coat, then arrange on the tart.

2. Black Currant Pyramid (page 52)

Presentation
Give the pears a golden color by brushing with coffee syrup (see translator's notes).

Technique
Chill the pyramid after unmolding so the glaze will adhere. Apply the glaze with a small off-set spatula.

3. Crème Brulée with Black Currants (p. 53)

Presentation
To caramelize the sugar evenly, use a torch to melt the sugar.

4. Black Currant Log Cake (p. 54)

Presentation
Use a torch to brown the meringue.

Technique
To make each slice of cake attractive, sprinkle the black currants evenly through the center of the mousse.

Ingredients
The "bûche" can be made in many flavors.

Orange Desserts

1. Orange Cream with Chocolate (p. 56)

Presentation
Make the chocolate disks as thin as possible. Arrange the orange sections in a circular pattern.

Technique
Assemble the dessert just before serving.

2. Orange Dome (p.57)

Presentation
Place the orange slices in a neat pattern to make an attractive presentation.

Technique
Add the chocolate decoration just before serving.

Ingredients
A fruit coulis or caramel sauce can replace the chocolate sauce.

3. Chocolate "Pavé" with Orange (p. 58)

Presentation
Same advice as for the Black Raspberry Pavé. Carefully blend the two sauces to make an attractive design.

Technique
Moisten the cake thoroughly with syrup.

Ingredients
The sauces can be applied in different patterns.

4. Orange Log Cake (p.59)

Presentation
Prop one slice of cake onto the other to give a little height to the dessert.

Technique advice
Make sure the cake is thoroughly chilled and firm before adding the jelly glaze.

Ingredients
Chocolate sauce can replace the caramel sauce.

Lemon Desserts

1. Lemon Tart (p. 61)

Presentation
Use a channel cutter to make a design around the edge of the lemon slices.

Technique
Coat the top lightly with glaze.

2. Lemon "Pavé" with Raspberry Coulis (p. 62)

Presentation
Same advice as for the Blackberry Pavé. Add the fruit garnish in a pretty pattern. Carefully swirl a little crème fraîche into the coulis.

Technique
Thoroughly moisten the cake with syrup. Sprinkle the top lightly and evenly with cocoa before glazing.

Ingredients
Other fruits could be used as garnish and to make the coulis.

3. Lemon Mousse with Tea-infused Caramel (p. 63)

Presentation
Coat only the top of the "tear drop" without letting the glaze drip down the sides. Use just a little caramel sauce.

Technique
Blend the chopped nougatine evenly into the mousse.

Ingredients
The chocolate decoration is optional.

Apple

1. Granny Smith Mousse with Blackberry Coulis (p. 66)

Presentation
Glaze the apples without dripping glaze down the sides. Spoon the coulis on the plate in an irregular pattern.

Technique
Granny Smith apples will give the best results.

Ingredients
The chocolate decoration is optional.

2. Apple Tart with Calvados Sabayon (p. 67)

Presentation
The top of the chibouste cream can be browned under the broiler.
Cover the bottom of the plate with sabayon.

Technique
Puff pastry trimmings can be used for the tart shells. Make the chibouste cream at the last minute.

Ingredients
Pears, apricots or raspberries can replace the apples.

3. Granny Smith Sorbet with Sugar Leaves (p. 68)

Presentation
Make the sugar leaves as thin as possible. Cook the apple slices until well caramelized.

Technique
The sorbet can be made in advance, scooped and stored in the freezer.

Ingredients
This dessert could be made with raspberry sorbet, with red color added to the sugar leaves. Serve with vanilla crème anglaise.

Apple Desserts

Pear Desserts

Cherry,

4. Apple Napoleon with Raspberry Caramel Sauce (p. 69)

Presentation
Place the apple slices so they can be seen and color the sugar lightly with red.

Technique
Bake the pastry layers until golden and very crisp. Apply the cream with a pastry bag.

Ingredients
Instead of the spun sugar, caramelize the top by covering with sugar and carefully melting with a torch.

5. Apple Brochettes Flamed with Calvados (p. 70)

Presentation
Brown the top of the dessert evenly either under the broiler or with a torch.

Technique
Flame the dessert just before serving, or at the table.

Ingredients
The brochettes can be made with a mixture of fresh seasonal fruits.

6. Apple Log Cake (p. 71)

Presentation
Same advice for plate presentation as the Orange Log Cake.

Technique
Arrange the slices of apples in a neat layer in the center of the mousse so that each slice looks the same.

Ingredients
Log cakes can be made in many flavors.

1. Pear Mousse (p. 73)

Presentation
Brush the pears with coffee syrup to give a golden color. Sprinkle powdered sugar on the chocolate decorations.

Technique
Thoroughly moisten the cake with syrup. Sprinkle the top lightly and evenly with cocoa before glazing.

Ingredients
The coulis can be replaced by chocolate sauce.

2. Pear Tart (p. 74)

Presentation
Fan the pear slices evenly in a rosette and glaze lightly with melted jelly.

Ingredients
This tart can be made with apricots, peaches or plums.

3. Pear Tart with Chocolate (p. 75)

Presentation
Place the chocolate decorations in a fan pattern and cover the ends with the chocolate truffle.

Technique
Chill the tarts in the refrigerator. Avoid moving the tarts while the ganache is setting so that the surface of the tarts remains smooth.

Ingredients
The tart can be made without the pears.

4. Pear Dome (p. 76)

Presentation
Brush a little coffee syrup on the pears to give them a golden color before brushing with jelly glaze. Apply the chocolate glaze with a paper cone.

Technique
After the molds are lined with pear slices, place in the freezer briefly before filling with cream.

Ingredients
A coulis could be ladled on the plate instead of applying the sauce with the paper cone.

5. Pear Gratin with Ginger (p. 77)

Presentation
Same advice as the Apple Brochettes.

Technique
Assemble the dessert just before serving.

Ingredients
The pears can be replaced with other fruits.

1. Black Forest Cake (p.79)

Presentation
Place the cherries in an even layer so that each portion has cherries showing.

Technique
Moisten the cake thoroughly with syrup. Apply an even, but not too thick, layer of whipped cream.

Ingredients
The layer of whipped cream can be replaced with chocolate mousse.

2. Cherry Bavarian Cream (p. 80)

Presentation
Alternate 3 cherries with 3 chocolate decorations. Add just a little sauce.

Technique
Coat the dessert lightly with jelly glaze without dripping it down the sides.

Ingredients
The white chocolate decorations can be made with dark chocolate.

3. Pineapple Meringue Tart (p. 81)

Presentation
Use a torch to brown the meringue.

Technique
Coat the top of the dessert without dripping glaze on the sides.

Ingredients
The meringue can be eliminated and the top simply coated with jelly glaze.

Pineapple and Grape *Desserts*

1. "Africa" (p. 82)

Presentation
Fan the chocolate curls around the dessert and cover the ends with the pieces of pineapple. Use a paper cone to pipe the decoration.

Technique
Make each layer very neat and uniform.

Ingredients
The glaze piped though the paper cone can be replaced by a fruit coulis spooned on the plate.

2. Chocolate Triangles with Cherries (p. 83)

Presentation
Make the chocolate triangles as thin as possible. Use just a little crème anglaise. Arrange the cherries so they can be seen.

Technique
Assemble the triangles and mousse filling first, then transfer to the plates.

Ingredients
The chocolate can be shaped into rectangles, circles or ovals.

3. Babas with Grapes and Muscat Sabayon (p. 84)

Presentation
Cut the cakes on the bias to best display the grapes. Arrange the garnishes in an attractive pattern.

Babas, cont.

Technique
Soak the babas while still warm so they absorb the syrup quickly to the center. There should be no dry portions of cake.

Ingredients
Various liqueurs can be used to flavor the babas. Match the fruit garnish to the flavor of the liqueur.

4. Chocolate Leaves with Grapes (p. 85)

Presentation
Make the circles of chocolate very thin. Place the grapes so they can be seen. Spoon the coulis on just part of the plate.

Technique
Use lightly whipped cream. Assemble the dessert, then transfer to the plate.

Ingredients
The whipped cream can be replaced with a mixture of pastry cream and whipped cream.

5. Pineapple "Pavé" with Mango Coulis (p. 86)

Presentation
Use a paper cone to decorate the plate with the coulis. Brush a light coat of jelly glaze into the pineapple.

Technique
Don't make the layer of buttercream too thick.

Ingredients
The covering chocolate can be replaced by a chocolate glaze.

Tropical Fruit *Desserts*

1. "Ile Maurice" (p. 88)

Use a paper cone to decorate the plate with the coulis.
Arrange the fruits in an attractive pattern.

Technique
Coat the top lightly with glaze.

Ingredients
The mousse can be made with another tropical fruit.

2. Savarin with Tropical fruits (p. 89)

Presentation
Same advice as the Fresh Fruit Charlotte.

Technique
Soak the cakes thoroughly with the syrup so there are no dry parts of cake. Brush on a light coat of jelly glaze to make them shine.

Ingredients
The coconut sauce can be replaced by a coulis of another tropical fruit.

3. Mango Mousse with Tropical Fruits (p. 90)

Presentation
Same advice as the Fresh Fruit Charlotte. Use just a little passion fruit sauce on each plate. Break the chocolate disks into irregular pieces.

Technique
Sprinkle the top lightly and evenly with cocoa powder before applying the jelly glaze.

Mango Mousse, cont.

Ingredients
The passion fruit sauce can be replaced by a coulis of another tropical fruit.

4. Frozen Nougat Creole (p. 91)

Presentation
Place the slices of nougat to follow the contour of the plate. Arrange the fruits in an attractive pattern.

Technique
Sprinkle the top lightly and evenly with cocoa powder before applying the jelly glaze.

Ingredients
The chocolate disks can be replaced with crispy cookies ("croustillants").

5. Tropical Fruit Sorbet (p. 92)

Presentation
Prop the filo triangles on the scoops of sorbet and arrange the fruits around the sorbet in an attractive pattern.

Technique
The nougat should be very firm before it is sliced.

Ingredients
"Croustillants" can be used in place of the filo decorations.

Banana, Kiwi and Prune Desserts

1. Banana Dome (p. 96)

Presentation
Use a paper cone to decorate the plate with the coulis. Place the dome in the center of the plate and decorate very neatly.

Technique
Clean the molds with a cotton towel before applying the chocolate.
The chocolate design can be made with melted chocoalte drizzled with a brush if a patissier's spray gun is not available.

2. Banana Gratin (p. 97)

Presentation
Same advice as Apple brochettes with Cavados.

Technique
The dessert tastes best if the raisins have macerated a long time.

3. Caramelized Bananas with Rum Sabayon (p. 98)

Presentation
Use tiny bananas if available for a more attractive presentation.

Technique
Bake the bananas in the oven until soft and caramelized.

4. Pear and Kiwi Mousse (p. 99)

Presentation
Cut the peeled kiwis lengthwise. Arrange the mousse, garnish and the two sauces by side on the plate.

5. Frozen Coconut Mousse with Raspberry Caramel Sauce (p. 100)

Presentation
Use a spoon to drizzle the sauce in a spiral on the plate.

Frozen Coconut Mousse, cont.

Ingredients
The caramel sauce can be replaced by a fruit coulis.

6. Kiwi Tart (p. 101)

Presentation
Cut the slices in half and overlap in a neat rosette.

Ingredients
The tart can be accompanied by a sauce.

7. Prune Tart (p. 102)

Presentation
Ladle just enough crème anglaise to cover the bottom of the plate. Decorate the plate with prunes placed neatly around the edge.

Ingredients
The crème anglaise can be replaced with a sabayon made with Armagnac.

8. "Far Breton" (p. 103)

Presentation
Choose a rustic earthenware baking dish to cook the "Far".

Technique
The top of the Far Breton can be brushed with jelly glaze to make it shine.

9. Armagnac Parfait with Prune Coulis (p. 104)

Presentation
Spoon the coulis around the edge of the plate. Place the decorations at even intervals around the parfait.

Technique
Assemble the dessert just before serving.

Chestnut Desserts

1. "Bûche Solognote" (p. 106)

Presentation
The chocolate glaze should be as thin as possible. Prop one slice of cake on the other to give dimension to the presentation.

Technique
Don't slice the cake until the glaze is set.

Ingredients
Instead of glazing the "bûche" with chocolate, the mold can be lined with sponge cake decorated with a wood grain design (see translator's notes).

2. Chestnut Mice (p. 107)

Presentation
Place the "mice" on one side of the plate and place the "cheese" on the other.

Technique
Chill the mice until they are very firm before dipping in the melted chocolate.

Ingredients
The mice can be dipped in a brown candy coating instead of a covering chocolate.

3. Chestnut Ice Cream (p. 108)

Presentation
The decorations for this dessert should look as authentically "woodsy" as possible. Chocolate "twigs" are made in France and add a realistic touch.

Pistachio and

1. Pistachio Bavarian Cream (p. 110)

Presentation
Arrange the chocolate disks to follow the contour of the plate. Brush a little jelly glaze on the pistachios to make them shine. Spoon just a little crème anglaise on the plates.

Technique
Chill the dessert after molding to firm the surface so that the jelly glaze will adhere better.

Ingredients
The bavarian can be molded into other forms.

2. Nut Lover's Dream (p. 111)

Presentation
Arrange the garnishes in a very neat pattern and lightly brush the hazelnuts with glaze to make them shine. Add just a drop of coffee syrup to swirl into the glaze.

Technique
Spoon the sauce on the plate before placing the dessert.

Ingredients
The caramel sauce can be replaced by a crème anglaise.

3. Pistachio Tuiles with Caramelized Apricots (p. 112)

Presentation
Same advice as "Croustillants" with Red Fruits.

Technique
Cook the apricots at a high enough heat to caramelize the sugar.

166

Hazelnut *Desserts*

4. Pistachio Pavé with Three Sauces (p. 113)

Presentation
Choose the most attractive slice of cake to place on the top of the pavé. Spoon the sauces on the plate in a pretty pattern, alternating the colors.

5. "Le Piémontais" (p. 114)

Presentation
Overlap the chocolate disks, arranging them to follow the shape of the plate. Blend the sauces to make an abstract design.

Technique
Chill the dessert thoroughly so that it can slice neatly.

Ingredients
Alternatively, this dessert can be finished with a dusting of cocoa.

6. "Squirrel's Delight" (p. 115)

Presentation
Prop the chocolate triangles against the scoops of ice cream. Press the nougatine against the chocolate.

Technique
Brush a little jelly glaze on the hazelnuts to make them shine.

Ingredients
The striped chocolate triangles can be replaced with dark chocolate disks.

Walnut and Almond

1. "Délice du Perigord" (p. 117)

Presentation
Arrange the chocolate triangles in pairs on the plate. Swirl a little coffee syrup into the crème anglaise.

Technique
Brush a little jelly glaze on the walnuts to make them shine.

2. "Sarlat" (p. 118)

Presentation
Place a walnut half on each nougatine rectangle. Use just a little caramel sauce.

Technique
Press the crumbled nougatine on top of the dessert as soon as it comes out of the freezer.

Ingredients
The caramel sauce can be replaced by crème anglaise.

3. "Amandine" (p. 119)

Presentation
Serve this dessert on a small plate.

Ingredients
The tart can be made without the raspberry jam.

4. "Blanc Manger" (p. 120)

Presentation
Spoon the raspberry coulis over the blanc manger so it drips down the sides. Arrange the three elements of the dessert separately on the plate.

Technique
Bake the puff pastry until golden and very crispy.

1. Chocolate Leaves with Mousse and Hazelnut Meringue (p. 126)

Presentation
Sprinkle a little cocoa powder on the crème anglaise. Arrange the chocolate "leaves" around the the edge of the plate.

Technique
Assemble the dessert just before serving.

2. Chocolate "Pavé" with Coffee Crème Anglaise (p. 127)

Presentation
Sprinkle the dark chocolate decorations with powdered sugar to give contrast.

Technique
Chill the pavé until very firm before slicing.

---

5. "Duguesclin" (p. 121)

Presentation
Arrange the chocolate decorations in order of size. Cover the top of the dessert with a generous "dusting" of powdered sugar.

Technique
Use a spatula to make the cream very smooth.

6. Walnut Ice Cream with "Croustillants" (p. 122)

Presentation
Same advice as "Croustillants" with Red Fruits. Spoon a little caramel sauce over the scoops of ice cream.

Ingredients
The chocolate decoration is optional.

Chocolate *Desserts*

3. Chocolate Mousse (p. 128)

Presentation
Serve the chocolate mousse in beautiful glasses.

4. "Profiteroles" (p. 129)

Presentation
Mound the profiteroles in the center of the plate and drizzle the warm chocolate sauce down the sides.

Technique
Keep the chocolate sauce warm in a water bath until the dessert is assembled.

5. Chocolate Mousse with Grand Marnier Sabayon (p. 130)

Presentation
Place the mousse in the center and spoon the sabayon around.

Technique
Allow the mousse to defrost just a little before pressing on the chocolate decorations.

6. Chocolate Pear "Bûche" (p. 131)

Presentation
Same advice as "Bûche Solognote".

Technique
Same advice as "Bûche Solognote".

Ingredients
Same advice as "Bûche Solognote".

Coffee Desserts

Vanilla and

1. **Coffee Charlotte with Apricot Coulis** (p. 133)

Presentation
Place the apricot halves to follow the contour of the plate. Pipe the sauces with a paper cone in the form of a tear drop.

Ingredients
The apricot coulis can be replaced by an apricot caramel sauce.

2. **"Moka"** (p. 134)

Presentation
Place the Moka on one side of the plate. Prop the chocolate disks to give height to the dessert. Swirl a little coffee syrup into the crème anglaise.

Technique
Moisten the cake thoroughly with syrup.

Ingredients
The decoration can be changed to be more "classical".

3. **Nougatine "Succés"** (p. 135)

Presentation
Spoon a thin ribbon of crème anglaise around the edge of the plate.

Technique
Use a spatula dipped in warm water to smooth the surface of the buttercream.

4. **"Equator"** (p. 136)

Presentation
Place the chocolate decorations on one half of the "pavé".

168

1. **Crème Caramel with Orange Sauce** (p. 139)

Presentation
Place the chocolate disks on the dessert just before serving.

Ingredients
The chocolate disks are optional.

2. **Pear and Caramel Charlotte** (p. 140)

Presentation
Alternate the pear slices and rectangles of nougatine. Add just a little chocolate decoration for contrast.

Technique
Coat the top of the charlotte with jelly glaze marbled with coffee syrup.

Ingredients
The caramel sauce can be replaced by a chocolate sauce.

(Coffee Desserts cont.)

Technique
Chill the pavé until very firm before slicing.

5. **Rum Raisin and Coffee Bombe** (p. 137)

Presentation
The glaze on the dome should be lightly marbled with coffee syrup. Place the chocolate fans at even intervals around the dessert.

Technique
Return the bombe to the freezer after unmolding to firm the surface before applying the Coffee Desserts

3. **Caramel Ice Cream "Tart"** (p. 141)

Presentation
Garnish the ice cream with a lot of nuts to give an "abundant" look to the dessert.

Technique
Assemble the dessert just before serving.

4. **Dessert for Gourmands** (p. 142)

Presentation
Place the three desserts on separate sides of the plate and divide the plate with a caramel sauce drizzled with a spoon.

Technique
Sprinkle the top of the chocolate mousse with powdered sugar before placing it on the plate.

5. **"Five O'Clock"** (p. 143)

Presentation
Assemble the dessert on the nougatine base and place to one side of the plate. Use just a little caramel sauce.

Technique
Keep the frozen mousse in the freezer until service.

1. **Hazelnut Sablées with Vanilla Cream** (p. 145)

Presentation
Assemble the cookies and cream in order of size, staggering them a little to give a curved form to the dessert.

Technique
Bake the sablée cookies until crisp but not too brown.

2. **Vacherin with Raspberry Coulis** (p. 146)

Presentation
Place the baked meringue ("vacherin") in the center of the plate.
Arrange the fruits in an attractive pattern.

Technique
Toast the sliced almonds until golden brown.

Ingredients
The vacherin can be filled with any flavor ice cream.

3. **Floating Island with Black Currant Caramel Sauce** (p. 147)

Presentation
Drizzle the caramel sauce evenly over the meringues. Make the sugar "cage" the same diameter as the serving dish.

Technique
The sugar cages will not keep well. Store in an air-tight container.

Ingredients
The caramel sauce can be flavored with other fruits.

Praline Desserts

4. Almond "Succés" (p. 148)

Presentation
Arrange the portion of "succés" on the plate so the layers are showing.

Technique
Smooth the surface of the buttercream with a warm spatula.

Ingredients
The plain meringue layer can be replaced by a third almond meringue.

5. Praline Dome with Rum Sabayon (p. 149)

Presentation
Spoon a thin ribbon of sabayon around the plate. The decorations should be minimal and very neat.

Technique
Return the dome to the freezer after unmolding to firm the surface before applying the glaze.

6. Praline Cream Puffs (p. 150)

Presentation
Place the puffs "2 by 2". Sprinkle a little cocoa powder on the crème anglaise.

Technique
Pipe the whipped cream just before serving for the best results.

Desserts made with "Fromage Blanc", Mint, Licorice or Coconut

1. Fresh Cheese Mousse with Nougatine (p. 152)

Presentation
Place the two "tear drop" shaped forms on the plate to form a heart. The decorations should be minimal and very neat.

Technique
The "tear drops" can be made ahead, covered and stored in the freezer.

Ingredients
The coulis can be made with another fruit.

2. Fresh Cheese Mousse with Red Fruits (p. 154)

Presentation
Same advice as "Vacherin".

Technique
The whipped cream used to decorate should be lightly whipped and smooth.

3. Mint "Pavé" (p. 154)

Presentation
Use a paper cone to pipe a neat and decorative design with the chocolate glaze and green-tinted jelly glaze.

Technique
Make the design on the plate before placing the portion of pavé on the plate.

Ingredients
The chocolate and jelly design on the plate can be replaced by a coulis or crème anglaise.

4. Mint Granité in a Chocolate Cup (p. 155)

Presentation
Place the cup in the center of the plate Spoon the coulis in a thin ribbon around the plate and place the red fruit garnish in an attractive pattern.

Technique
Add the scoop of mint granité just before serving.

5. Chocolate Licorice Tart (p. 156)

Presentation
Serve the tart on a small plate and spoon a little crème anglaise around the tart.

Technique
While the tarts are chilling in the refrigerator, avoid moving them in any way so that the ganche remains very smooth as it sets.

Ingredients
The layer of sponge cake is optional.

6. Frozen Licorice Parfait (p. 157)

Presentation
Assemble the parfait on the nougatine base and place on one side of the plate. Swirl a little chocolate glaze into the crème anglaise.

technique
Assemble the dessert just before serving.

7. "Bermuda Triangle" (p. 158)

Presentation
Arrange the fruits in a natural pattern, making the most of the shapes and colors. Place the triangle on one side of the plate and coat lightly with coconut sauce.

Technique
Chill the mousse after unmolding so the surface is firm and cold before glazing.

8. "Souvenir from the Islands" (p. 159)

Presentation
Arrange the fruits in a natural pattern, making the most the the shapes and colors. Place the "coconut" at an angle. Add a light coat of passion fruit sauce.

Technique
To hold the chocolate "shells" on the plate, Place the shell on a hot surface long enough to melt the center a little. Transfer immediately to the plate and allow the melted spot to adhere to plate.

Preparation and Storage Chart

Preparation Time
x x x Long preparation
x x Average preparation
x Quick to prepares

Degree of Difficulty
x x x Difficult, for experienced chefs
x x Average difficulty
x Easy, no experience needed

Cost
x x x High cost in ingredients/labor
xx Average cost
x Economical

Freezer Storage
YES Can be made ahead and frozen
NO Freezing is not recommended

Page	DESSERTS *(by group)*	PREPARATION/STORAGE				DECORATIONS AND GARNISHES				
		Preparation Time	Difficulty	Cost	Freezer Storage	Fruit Garnish	Chocolate Decoration	Cooked Sugar Decoration	Jelly Glaze Decorations	Pastry and Cake Decorations
	FRESH FRUIT *Desserts*									
38	Fresh Fruit Charlotte	x x	x x	x	**YES**	☆	–	–	☆	☆
39	Harlequin Tart	x	x	x	**NO**	☆	–	–	☆	–
40	«Croustillants»	x	x	x	**NO**	☆	–	–	–	☆
41	Fresh Fruits in Crispy Pastry	x	x	x	**NO**	☆	–	–	☆	☆
42	Warm Apricot Tart	x	x	x	**NO**	☆	–	–	☆	–
43	Peach and Almond Delight	x x	x	x x	**YES**	☆	–	–	☆	☆
	RED FRUIT *Desserts*									
45	Raspberry «Croustillants» with Red Fruits	x	x	x	**NO**	☆	–	–	–	☆
46	Raspberry Dome	x x	x	x x	**YES**	☆	–	–	☆	–
47	Red Fruit Tart	x	x	x x	**NO**	☆	–	–	☆	–
48	Blackberry Pavé	x x	x x	x	**YES**	☆	–	–	☆	☆
49	Napoleon with Strawberries	x x x	x x	x x	**NO**	☆	–	–	☆	–
	BLACK CURRANT *Desserts*									
51	Almond Tart with Black Currants	x	x	x	**NO**	☆	–	–	☆	–
52	Black Currant Pyramid	x x x	x x x	x x	**YES**	☆	–	–	☆	–
53	Crème Brulée with Black Currants	x	x	x	**NO**	☆	–	–	☆	–
54	Black Currant Log Cake	x x	x	x	**YES**	☆	–	–	–	☆

Types of Decorations used for «Designer» Desserts

This table outlines the types of decorations used for each dessert as described in the beginning of the book :

1. Fruit garnish
2. Chocolate decoration
3. Cooked sugar decoration
4. Jelly glaze decoration/coating
5. Pastry and cake decorations

Type of mixtures and batters used in each dessert

The following table outlines for easy reference the types of mixtures, grouped in 9 categories, used to prepare each dessert. The recipes for these mixtures and batters are included in a separate chapter.

Page	DESSERTS *(by group)*	MIXTURES AND BATTERS USED TO MAKE EACH DESSERTS								
		1. Creamy mixtures	2. Ganaches	3. Mousses	4. Various fillings	5. Frozen preparations	6. Sauces	7. Pastries	8. Cakes and baked meringues	9. Various mixtures
	FRESH FRUIT *Desserts*									
38	Fresh Fruit Charlotte	●	–	–	–	–	●	–	●	●
39	Harlequin Tart	●	–	–	–	–	–	●	●	●
40	«Croustillants»	●	–	–	–	–	●	–	–	●
41	Fresh Fruits in Crispy Pastry	●	–	–	–	–	●	–	–	–
42	Warm Apricot Tart	–	–	–	–	–	–	●	–	●
43	Peach and Almond Delight	–	–	●	–	–	●	–	●	●
	RED FRUIT *Desserts*									
45	Raspberry Croustillants with Red Fruits	●	–	–	–	–	●	–	–	●
46	Raspberry Dome	–	–	●	–	–	●	●	●	●
47	Red Fruit Tart	●	–	–	–	–	●	●	●	●
48	Blacberry Pavé	–	–	●	–	–	●	–	●	●
49	Napoleon with Strawberries	●	–	–	–	–	●	●	–	●
	BLACK CURRANT *Desserts*									
51	Almond Tart with Black Currants	●	–	–	–	–	–	●	–	●
52	Black Currant Pyramid	–	–	●	–	–	●	–	●	●
53	Crème Brulée with Black Currants	●	–	–	–	–	–	–	–	–
54	Black Currant Log Cake	–	–	●	☆	–	●	–	●	●

Page	DESSERTS (by group)	PREPARATION/STORAGE				DECORATIONS AND GARNISHES				
		Preparation Time	Difficulty	Cost	Freezer Storage	Fruit Garnish	Chocolate Decoration	Cooked Sugar Decoration	Jelly Glaze Decoration	Pastry and Cake Decorations
	ORANGE *Desserts*									
56	Orange Cream with Chocolate	x	x	x	**NO**	☆	☆	–	–	–
57	Orange Dome	x x x	x x	x x	**YES**	☆	–	–	☆	–
58	Chocolate Pavé with Orange	x x	x x	x x	**YES**	☆	☆	–	☆	–
59	Orange Log Cake	x x x	x x	x x	**YES**	☆	☆	–	☆	–
	LEMON *Desserts*									
61	Lemon Tart	x	x	x	**NO**	☆	–	–	☆	–
62	Lemon Pavé with Raspberry Coulis	x	x x x	x	**YES**	☆	–	–	☆	–
63	Lemon Mousse with Tea-Infused Caramel	x x x	x x x	x x x	**YES**	☆	☆	–	☆	☆
	APPLE *Desserts*									
66	Granny Smith Mousse with Blackberry Coulis	x x x	x x x	x x x	**YES**	☆	☆	–	☆	–
67	Apple Tart with Calvados Sabayon	x x	x x	x	**NO**	–	–	–	–	–
68	Granny Smith Sorbet with Sugar Leaves	x x	x x	x x	**YES**	☆	–	☆	–	–
69	Apple «Millefeuille» with Raspberry Caramel Sauce	x x x	x x	x x x	**NO**	☆	–	☆	–	–
70	Apple Brochette Flamed with Calvados	x	x	x	**NO**	☆	–	–	–	–
71	Apple Log Cake	x x x	x x	x x x	**YES**	☆	☆	–	☆	☆
	PEAR *Desserts*									
73	Pear Mousse	x x x	x x	x x	**YES**	☆	☆	–	☆	☆
74	Pear Tart	x	x	x	**NO**	☆	–	–	☆	–
75	Pear Tart with Chocolate	x x x	x x	x x	**NO**	–	☆	–	–	–
76	Per Dome	x x x	x x	x x	**YES**	☆	☆	–	☆	–
77	Pear Gratin with Ginger	x	x	x	**NO**	☆	–	–	–	–

(Continued)

Page	DESSERTS *(by group)*	1. Creamy mixtures	2. Ganaches	3. Mousses	4. Various fillings	5. Frozen preparations	6. Sauces	7. Pastries	8. Cakes an baked meringues	9. Various mixtures
	MIXTURES AND BATTERS USED TO MAKE EACH DESSERT									
	ORANGE *Desserts*									
56	Orange Cream with Chocolate	●	–	–	–	–	●	–	–	–
57	Orange Dome	●	–	–	–	–	●	–	●	●
58	Chocolate Pavé with Orange	●	●	–	–	–	●	–	●	●
59	Orange Log Cake	●	–	–	–	–	–	–	●	●
	LEMON *Desserts*									
61	Lemon Tart	●	–	–	–	–	–	●	–	●
62	Lemon Pavé with Raspberry Coulis	●	–	–	–	–	●	–	●	●
63	Lemon Mousse with Tea-Infused Caramel	–	●	●	–	–	●	–	●	●
	APPLE *Desserts*									
66	Granny Smith Mousse with Blackberry Coulis	–	–	●	–	–	●	●	●	●
67	Apple Tart with Calvados Sabayon	●	–	–	–	–	●	●	–	–
68	Granny Smith Sorbet with Sugar Leaves	–	–	–	–	●	●	–	–	–
69	Apple «Millefeuille» with Raspberry Caramel Sauce	●	–	–	–	–	●	●	–	–
70	Apple Brochette Flamed with Calvados	–	–	–	●	–	–	–	–	–
71	Apple Log Cake	–	–	●	–	–	●	–	●	●
	PEAR *Desserts*									
73	Pear Mousse	–	–	●	●	–	●	–	●	●
74	Pear Tart	●	–	–	–	–	–	●	–	–
75	Pear Tart with Chocolate	–	●	–	–	–	●	●	–	●
76	Pear Dome	●	–	–	–	–	–	–	●	●
77	Pear Gratin with Ginger	–	–	–	●	–	–	–	–	●

Page	**DESSERTS** *(by group)*	PREPARATION/STORAGE				DECORATIONS AND GARNISHES				
		Preparation Time	Difficulty	Cost	Freezer Storage	Fruit Garnish	Chocolate Decoration	Cooked Sugar Decoration	Jelly Glaze Decoration	Pastry and Cake Decorations
	MADE WITH PINEAPPLE, CHERRIES, GRAPES *Desserts*									
79	Black Forest Cake	x x	x	x x	**NO**	–	☆	–	–	–
80	Cherry Bavarian Cream	x x	x x x	x x	**YES**	☆	☆	–	☆	–
81	Pineapple Meringue Tart	x	x x	x	**NO**	–	–	–	–	☆
82	Africa	x x x	x x x	x x x	**YES**	☆	☆	–	☆	–
83	Chocolate Triangles with Cherries	x x	x x x	x x	**NO**	–	☆	–	–	–
84	Babas with Grapes and Muscat Sabayon	x x x	x x x	x	**NO**	☆	–	–	☆	☆
85	Chocolate Leaves with Grapes	x	x x	x x	**NO**	☆	☆	–	–	–
86	Pineapple Pavé with Mango Coulis	x x	x x	x x	**YES**	☆	☆	–	☆	–
	TROPICAL FRUIT *Desserts*									
88	Ile Maurice	x x	x x x	x x	**YES**	☆	☆	–	☆	☆
89	Savarin with Tropical Fruits	x x x	x x x	x x	**NO**	☆	–	–	☆	–
90	Mango Mousse with Tropical Fruits	x x	x x	x x	**YES**	☆	☆	–	☆	–
91	Frozen Nougat Creole	x x	x x	x x	**YES**	☆	☆	–	–	–
92	Tropical Fruit Sorbet	x	x x	x	**YES**	☆	–	–	–	☆
	MADE WITH BANANAS, KIWIS, PRUNES *Desserts*									
96	Banana Dome	x x	x x x	x x	**YES**	☆	☆	–	–	–
97	Banana Gratin	x	x	x	**NO**	☆	–	–	–	–
98	Caramelized Bananas with Rum Sabayon and Coconut Sorbet	x	x	x x	**NO**	☆	–	–	–	–
99	Pear and Kiwi Mousse	x x	x x	x	**YES**	☆	☆	–	☆	–
100	Rasbperry Caramel Sauce	x x	x	x	**YES**	☆	–	–	–	–
101	Kiwi Tart	x	x	x	**NO**	☆	–	–	☆	–
102	Prune Tart	x	x	x x	**NO**	☆	–	–	☆	–
103	«Far breton»	x	x	x	**NO**	–	–	–	–	–
104	Armagnac Parfait with Prune Coulis	x x	x x	x x	**YES**	☆	☆	–	–	–

(Continued)

MIXTURES AND BATTERS USED TO MAKE EACH DESSERTS

Page	DESSERTS (by group)	1. Creamy mixtures	2. Ganaches	3. Mousses	4. Various fillings	5. Frozen preparations	6. Sauces-	7. Pastries	8. Cakes and baked meringues	9. Various mixtures
	MADE WITH PINEAPPLE, CHERRIES, GRAPES *Desserts*									
79	Black Forest Cake	●	–	–	–	–	●	–	●	–
80	Cherry Bavarian Cream	●	–	–	–	–	●	–	●	●
81	Pineapple Meringue Tart	–	–	–	●	–	–	●	●	●
82	Africa	●	–	●	–	–	–	–	●	●
83	Chocolate Triangles with Cherries	–	–	●	–	–	●	–	–	–
84	Babas with Grapes and Muscat Sabayon	●	–	–	–	–	●	●	–	●
85	Chocolate Leaves with Grapes	●	–	–	–	–	●	–	–	–
86	Pineapple Pavé with Mango Coulis	●	–	–	–	–	●	–	●	●
	TROPICAL FRUIT *Desserts*									
88	Ile Maurice	–	–	●	–	–	●	–	●	●
89	Savarin with Tropical Fruits	–	–	–	–	–	●	●	–	●
90	Mango Mousse with Tropical Fruits	–	–	●	–	–	●	–	●	●
91	Frozen Nougat Creole	–	–	–	–	●	●	–	–	–
92	Tropical Fruit Sorbet	–	–	–	–	●	●	–	–	–
	MADE WITH BANANAS, KIWIS, PRUNES *Desserts*									
96	Banana Dome	–	–	●	–	–	●	–	●	–
97	Banana Gratin	–	–	–	●	–	–	–	–	–
98	Caramelized Bananas with Rum Sabayon and Coconut Sorbet	–	–	–	–	●	●	–	–	–
99	Pear and Kiwi Mousse	–	–	●	–	–	●	–	●	●
100	Raspberry Caramel Sauce	–	–	–	–	●	●	–	–	–
101	Kiwi Tart	●	–	–	–	–	–	●	–	–
102	Prune Tart	●	–	–	–	–	●	●	–	●
103	«Far breton»	–	–	–	●	–	●	–	–	●
104	Armagnac Parfait with Prune Coulis	–	–	–	–	●	●	–	–	●

Page	DESSERTS *(by group)*	PREPARATION/STORAGE				DECORATIONS AND GARNISHES				
		Preparation Time	Difficulty	Cost	Freezer Storage	Fruit Garnish	Chocolate Decoration	Cooked Sugar Decoration	Jelly Glaze Decoration	Pastry and Cake Decorations
	CHESTNUT *Desserts*									
106	«Bûche Solognote»	x x x	x x	x x x	**YES**	☆	☆	☆	☆	—
107	Chestnut Mice	x x x	x x	x x x	**YES**	—	☆	—	—	—
108	Chestnut Ice Cream	x	x	x	**YES**	☆	☆	—	—	—
	PISTACHIO/HAZELNUT *Desserts*									
110	Pistachio Bavarian Cream	x x x	x x x	x x x	**YES**	☆	☆	—	☆	☆
111	Nut Lover's Dream	x x	x x x	x x	**YES**	☆	☆	—	☆	—
112	Pistachio Tuiles with Caramelized Apricots	x	x	x x	**NO**	☆	☆	—	—	—
113	Pistachio Pavé with Three Sauces	x x	x x	x x	**YES**	☆	☆	—	☆	☆
114	«Squirrel's Delight»	x x x	x x	x x x	**YES**	☆	☆	—	—	—
	WALNUT/ALMOND *Desserts*									
117	«Délice du Périgord»	x x	x x	x x	**YES**	☆	☆	—	☆	—
118	«Sarlat»	x x	x x	x x	**YES**	☆	☆	—	—	☆
119	«Amandine»	x	x	x	**NO**	—	—	—	☆	—
120	«Blanc-manger»	x x x	x x	x x	**YES**	☆	☆	—	—	—
121	«Duguesclin»	x	x	x x	**NO**	—	☆	—	—	—
122	Walnut Ice Cream with Croustillants	x x	x	x x	**YES**	—	☆	—	—	☆
	CHOCOLATE *Desserts*									
126	Chocolate Leaves with Mousse and Hazelnut Meringue	x x	x x	x x	**NO**	—	☆	—	—	—
127	Chocolate Pavé with Coffee Crème Anglaise	x x	x x	x x	**YES**	—	☆	—	—	—
128	Chocolate Mousse	x	x	x	**NO**	—	☆	—	—	☆
129	Profiteroles	x	x	x	**YES**	—	—	—	—	—
130	Chocolate Mousse with Grand-Marnier Sabayon	x x x	x x	x x x	**YES**	—	☆	—	☆	—
131	Chocolate and Pear «Bûches»	x x x	x x	x x	**YES**	☆	☆	—	☆	—

Page	DESSERTS *(by group)*	1. Creamy mixtures	2. Ganaches	3. Mousses	4. Various fillings	5. Frozen preparations	6. Sauces	7. Pastries	8. Cakes and baked meringues	9. Various mixtures
	MIXTURES AND BATTERS USED TO MAKE EACH DESSERT									
	CHESTNUT *Desserts*									
106	«Bûche Solognote»	●	–	–	–	–	●	–	●	●
107	Chestnut Mice	●	–	–x	–	–	●	●	–	●
108	Chestnut Ice Cream	–	–	–	–	●	●	–	–	–
	PISTACHIO/HAZELNUT *Desserts*									
110	Pistachio Bavarian Cream	●	–	–	—	–	●	–	●	●
111	Nut Lovers' Dream	●	–	●	–	–	●	–	●	●
112	Pistachio Tuiles with Caramelized Apricots	●	–	–	–	–	●	–	–	●
113	Pistachio Pavé with Three Sauces	●	–	–	–	–	●	–	●	●
114	«Squirrel's Delight»	●	–	–	–	–	●	–	●	–
	WALNUT/ALMOND *Desserts*									
117	«Délice du Périgord»	●	–	–	–	–	●	–	●	●
118	«Sarlat»	●	–	–	–	–	●	–	●	●
119	«Amandine»	●	–	–	–	–	●	●	–	●
120	«Blanc-manger»	–	–	–	●	–	●	●	–	–
121	«Duguesclin»	●	–	–	–	–	●	–	●	–
122	Walnut Ice Cream with Croustillants	–	–	–	–	●	●	–	–	●
	CHOCOLATE *Desserts*									
126	Chocolate Leaves with Mousse and Hazelnut Meringue	–	–	●	–	–	●	–	●	–
127	Chocolate Pavé with Coffee Crème Anglaise	–	●	–	–	–	●	–	●	–
128	Chocolate Mousse	–	–	●	–	–	–	–	–	●
129	Profiteroles	–	–	–	–	●	●	●	–	–
130	Chocolate Mousse with Grand-Marnier Sabayon	–	–	●	–	–	●	–	●	●
131	Chocolate and Pear «Bûches»	–	–	●	–	–	●	–	●	●

(Continued)

Page	DESSERTS *(by group)*	PREPARATION/STORAGE				DECORATIONS AND GARNISHES				
		Preparation Time	Difficulty	Cost	Freezer Storage	Fruit Garnish	Chocolate Decoration	Cooked Sugar Decoration	Jelly Glaze Decoration	Pastry and Cake Decorations
	COFFEE *Desserts*									
133	Coffee Charlotte with Apricot Coulis	x x x	x x x	x x	**YES**	☆	☆	–	☆	☆
134	«Moka»	x x	x x	x x	**NO**	–	☆	–	–	–
135	Nougatine «Succès»	x x	x x	x x	**NO**	–	☆	–	–	☆
136	«Equator»	x x	x x	x x	**NO**	–	☆	–	☆	–
137	Rum Raisin and Coffee Bombe	x x x	x x x	x x	**YES**	☆	☆	–	☆	–
	CARAMEL/TEA *Desserts*									
139	Crème Caramel with Orange Sauce	x	x	x	**NO**	–	☆	–	–	☆
140	Pear and Caramel Charlotte	x x x	x x x	x x x	**YES**	☆	☆	–	☆	☆
141	Caramel Tart	x x x	x x x	x x	**YES**	☆	–	–	–	☆
142	Dessert for «gourmands»	x x x	x x	x x x	**YES**	☆	–	–	–	☆
143	«Five O'Clock»	x x	x x	x x	**YES**	–	☆	–	–	☆
	VANILLA/PRALINE *Desserts*									
145	Hazelnut «Sablés» with Vanilla Cream	x x	x x	x	**NO**	☆	☆	–	–	–
146	Vacherin with Raspberry Coulis	x x	x x	x x	**YES**	☆	–	–	–	–
147	Floating Island with Blanc Currant Caramel Sauce	x x	x x	x	**NO**	–	–	☆	–	☆
148	Almond «Succès»	x	x	x x	**NO**	–	☆	–	–	–
149	Praline Dome with Rum Sabayon	x x	x x x	x	**YES**	–	☆	–	☆	☆
150	Praline Cream Puffs («Salambos»)	x x	x x	x	**NO**	–	☆	☆	–	–
	MADE WITH RICOTTA, MINT, LICORICE, COCONUT *Desserts*									
152	Fresh Cheese Mousse with Nougatine	x x x	x x x	x x	**YES**	☆	☆	–	☆	–
153	Fresh Cheese Mousse with Fruits and Chocolate	x x	x x	x x	**YES**	☆	–	–	–	☆
154	Mint Pavé	x x	x x	x	**YES**	☆	☆	–	☆	–
155	Mint Granité in a Chocolate Cup	x x x	x x x	x x	**YES**	☆	☆	–	–	–
156	Chocolate Licorice Tart	x x x	x	x x	**NO**	–	☆	–	–	–
157	Frozen Licorice Parfait	x x	x x	x x	**YES**	–	☆	–	☆	☆
158	«Bermuda Triangles»	x x x	x x	x x	**YES**	☆	☆	–	☆	–
159	«Souvenir from the Islands»	x x x	x x x	x x x	**YES**	☆	☆	–	–	–

(Continued)

Page	DESSERTS *(by group)*	MIXTURES AND BATTERS USED TO MAKE EACH DESSERT								
		1. Creamy mixtures	2. Ganaches	3. Mousses	4. Various fillings	5. Frozen preparations	6. Sauces	7. Pastries	8. Cakes and baked meringues	9. Various mixtures
	COFFEE *Desserts*									
133	Coffee Charlotte with Apricot Coulis	●	–	●	–	–	●	–	●	●
134	«Moka»	●	–	–	–	–	●	–	●	●
135	Nougatine «Succès»	●	–	–	–	–	●	–	●	●
136	«Equator»	●	–	–	–	–	●	–	●	–
137	Rum Raisin and Coffee Bombe	–	–	–	–	●	●	–	–	●
	CARAMEL/TEA *Desserts*									
139	Crème Caramel with Orange Sauce	●	–	–	–	–	●	–	–	●
140	Pear and Caramel Charlotte	●	–	●	–	–	●	–	●	●
141	Caramel Tart	–	–	–	–	●	●	–	–	●
142	Dessert for «gourmands»	–	–	–	–	●	●	–	–	●
143	«Five O'Clock»	–	–	–	–	●	●	–	–	●
	VANILLA/PRALINE *Desserts*									
145	Hazelnut «Sablés» with Vanilla Cream	●	–	–	–	–	●	●	–	–
146	Vacherin with Raspberry Coulis	●	–	–	–	●	●	–	●	●
147	Floating Island with Blanc Currant Caramel Sauce	–	–	–	–	–	●	–	–	●
148	Almond «Succès»	●	–	–	–	–	●	–	●	–
149	Praline Dome with Rum Sabayon	–	–	–	–	●	●	–	●	●
150	Praline Cream Puffs («Salambos»)	●	–	–	–	–	●	●	–	–
	MADE WITH RICOTTA, MINT, LICORICE, COCONUT *Desserts*									
152	Fresh Cheese Mousse with Nougatine	–	–	●	–	–	●	–	–	●
153	Fresh Cheese Mousse with Fruits and Chocolate	●	–	●	–	–	●	–	●	–
154	Mint Pavé	●	–	–	–	–	–	–	●	●
155	Mint granité in a Chocolate Cup	–	–	●	–	●	●	–	–	–
156	Chocolate Licorice Tart	–	●	–	–	–	●	●	●	●
157	Frozen Licorice Parfait	–	–	–	–	●	●	–	●	●
158	«Bermuda Triangle»	–	–	●	–	–	●	–	●	●
159	«Souvenir fron the Islands»	–	–	–	–	●	●	–	–	–

Basic Recipes used in French Patisserie

The desserts in this book combine many elements for a spectacular result. The classic recipes to make the various parts of these desserts are described in this section and are grouped in the following categories:

1. Creamy Mixtures

All of these mixtures (except "crème Chantilly" or whipped cream) contain eggs as either a thickener or as the main ingredient. The shelf life on many of these mixtures is very limited.

2. Ganaches

Ganache is made with cream and melted chocolate. It can be flavored or left plain and is used as an icing or a filling.

3. Mousses

These mixtures usually contain gelatin and professional French pastry chefs chill them quickly in the freezer until the gelatin sets. A combination of Italian meringue and whipped cream gives them a light, delicate texture. A well-made mousse will keep for several days.

4. "Bombe" Mixture and Italian Meringue

These two mixtures, one made with egg yolks, the other with egg whites combined with hot sugar syrup are used primarily in making mousses but are also used in other desserts.

5. Frozen Mixtures

These include ice cream, sorbet, frozen nougat and granité.

6. Sauces

A variety of sauces in a wide range of flavors and colors are used to augment the presentation and taste of desserts. "Coulis", or puréed fruit sauce can be made with almost any fruit.

7. Pastry

These include the classic recipes for pie pastry, puff pastry and cream puff dough.

8. Cakes and Baked Meringues

Thin layers of sponge cake in various flavors and crisp meringue are combined with creamy mixtures and mousses to assemble many of the desserts in this volume.

9. Various Mixture

This group includes glazes, decorations and other mixtures that do not fit into the other categories.

I - Creamy Mixtures
1. Vanilla Pastry Cream
2. Almond Cream
3. Buttercream
   "Flavorings for buttercream"
4. Whipped Cream
5. Lemon Filling
6. Lemon Mousseline
7. Praline Mousseline
8. Orange Filling
9. Light Orange Cream
10. Light Vanilla Cream
11. Light Pistachio Cream
12. Walnut Cream
13. "Duguesclin" Cream
14. Chiboust
15. Crème Brûlée
16. Crème Caramel
17. Bavarian Cream
   "Ten Variations for Bavarian Cream"

Basic Recipes for

II - Ganaches

1. Basic Ganache
2. Orange Ganache
3. Ganache for Tarts
4. Licorice Ganache for Tarts

III - Mousses

1. Hazelnut Mousse
2. Chocolate Mousse
3. Lemon Mousse
4. Fresh Cheese ("fromage blanc") Mousse
5. Fruit Mousse

IV - Various Mixtures

1. Italian Meringue
   "Which Meringue to Use?"
2. "Bombe" Mixture
3. Gratin Mixture
4. "Blanc-manger" Mixture
5. "Far Breton" Mixture

V - Frozen Preparations

1. Frozen Nougat Créole
2. Mint Granité
3. Frozen Coconut Mousse
4. Frozen Tea Mousse
5. Frozen "Parfait" (créole, rum, Armagnac, licorice)

Which Cream to Use?

Cream is an important ingredient in pastry making. But which cream is best for each recipe – "crème fraîche", whipping cream, light cream?

"Crème fraîche"
This thick, slightly acidic cream is more widely used and available in France where it is used in "cuisine" as well as "patisserie". Cold, it is used "as is" (not whipped) as an accompaniment, with Tart Tatin for example. It is excellent in sauces or mixtures that require boiling the cream. Heavy cream can be used in these cooked preparations if crème fraîche is not available.

Long Conservation Cream
In France, long conservation dairy products have been used more and more in recent years. They can be bought in quantity and don't need to be refrigerated. Since they are sterilized, there is less chance of spoilage once opened. This cream whips well, stands up to boiling and is good in cooked custards such as crème brulée.

Heavy Cream and Light Cream
In France, "crème fleurette" (fresh light cream) is a product lower in butterfat than crème fraîche but rich enough to be whipped. When a sauce or custard calls for cream, American light cream can be used but when whipped cream is called for, use heavy or whipping cream.

Designer Desserts

VI - Sauces

1. Fruit Coulis
   "Nine Variations for Fruit Coulis"

2. Crème anglaise (vanilla, coffee, pistachio, cinnamon)

3. Sabayon (rum, raspberry liqueur, Grand Marnier, Kirsch, Muscat, Calvados)

4. Caramel Sauce
   "Seven Variations of Caramel Sauce; Deglazing"

5. Various Sauces
   Coconut Sauce
   Cherry Sauce
   Passion Fruit Sauce
   Chocolate Sauce

VII - Pastries

1. Sweet Pie Pastry

2. Hazelnut Pie Pastry

3. Puff Pastry

4. Baba Dough

5. Cream Puff Dough

6. Ice cream (vanilla, coffee, praline, chestnut, caramel)
   "Seven Variations for Ice Cream"

7. Sorbets (coconut, mango, passion fruit, Granny smith)
   "Four Variations for Sorbets)

VIII - Cakes and Baked Meringues

1. Sponge cake

2. Chocolate Sponge cake

3. Almond Sponge cake

4. Ladyfingers

5. "Russe"

6. Orange Sponge cake

7. Coconut Sponge cake

8. Hazelnut or Coconut Meringue ("Dacquoise")

9. Almond Meringue ("Succés")

10. French Meringue

IX - Various Mixtures

1. Chocolate Cigarette Batter

2. Basic Cigarette Batter

3. Almond Brittle ("Nougatine")

4. Pineapple Filling

5. "Croustillants"
   "Four Recipes for "Croustillants"

6. Florentines

7. Jelly Glaze

8. Chocolate Glaze

9. Pears with Ginger

10. Grand Marnier Truffles

12. Simple Syrup for Imbibing Cakes
    "Twelve Flavorings for Simple Syrup"

1. Vanilla Pastry Cream

1 L (1 qt) whole milk
220 g (7 oz) sugar
8 egg yolks
90 g (3 oz) cornstarch
50 g (1 2/3 oz) unsalted butter
1/2 vanilla bean

Split the vanilla bean and scrape the inside with the tip of a knife. Add the bean and the "seeds" to the milk, add half the sugar and bring to a boil in a heavy saucepan.
Beat the egg yolks with the remaining sugar and the cornstarch
until light and lemon colored.
Whisk a little hot milk into the egg mixture. Return it to the saucepan and bring to a simmer; cook about 3 minutes until thick.
Remove from the heat and whisk in the butter. Transfer to a shallow dish and refrigerate to cool rapidly.

Shelf life: 24 hours in the refrigerator in a covered, non-reactive container.

2. Almond Cream

250 g (8 oz) unsalted butter
250 g (8 oz) sugar
250 g (8 oz) powdered almonds
4 large eggs
1/8 tsp vanilla extract
1/8 tsp rum

Cream the butter and sugar.
Stir in the powdered almonds.
Blend the eggs into the mixture until smooth.
Flavor the almond cream with vanilla and rum.

Shelf life: 1 week in the refrigerator in a covered, non-reactive container.

3. Buttercream

500 g (16 oz) sugar
150 ml (5 fl oz) water
8 egg yolks
750 g (1 lb 8 oz) unsalted butter
Flavoring (see below)

Mix the sugar and water in a heavy saucepan, cook to the soft ball stage (112 C (230 F)). Meanwhile, beat the yolks until light and lemon-colored. With the mixer running, slowly pour the cooked syrup into the yolks and continue beating until the mixture is cool.
Beat the butter (room-temperature) until creamy then whisk it gently into the cooled egg mixture.

Shelf life: 1 week in the refrigerator in a covered, non-reactive container.

Flavoring for 500 g (8 oz) buttercream	
Chestnut	300 g (10 oz) puréed, sweetened chestnuts and 20 ml (2/3 fl oz) rum
Praline	160 g (5 1/3 oz) crushed praline (almond brittle)
Hazelnut	200 g (6 1/2 oz) hazelnut butter
Rhum	30 ml (1 fl oz) rum
Coffee	15 ml (.5 fl oz) coffee syrup strong coffee

4. Whipped cream

500 ml whipping cream
75 g (2 1/2 oz) powdered sugar
1/8 tsp vanilla extract

Chill the bowl and whisk in the freezer.
Whip the cream in the chilled bowl to the desired consistency and whisk in the vanilla.
If using long-life cream, be sure to refrigerate 24 hours in advance.

Shelf life: Whip cream just before using for best results.

I - Creamy Mixtures *(continued)*

5. Lemon Curd

2 lemons, juice and zest
3 large eggs
150 g (5 oz) sugar
50 g (1 2/3 oz) unsalted butter, melted

Whisk together all the ingredients until smooth in the top of a double boiler. Cook over simmering water until the mixture bubbles and thickens, whisking constantly. Transfer to a shallow dish to cool rapidly.

Shelf life: 24 hours, refrigerated, covered, in a non-reactive container.

6. Lemon Mousseline

500 ml (8 fl oz) whole milk
3 egg yolks
160 g (5 1/3 oz) sugar
60 g (2 oz) cornstarch
300 g (10 oz) unsalted butter (creamed)
500 g (1 lb) lemon curd

Make a pastry cream with the milk, eggs, sugar and cornstarch.
Place the cooled pastry cream in a mixer and blend with a whisk until smooth. Slowly beat in the butter and lemon curd and blend until smooth. Use as a filling for layered cakes.

Shelf life: Store in a covered container in the freezer.

7. Praline Mousseline

500 g (1 lb) cold pastry cream
250 g (8 oz) unsalted butter (creamed)
125 g (4 oz) praline paste

Place the cooled pastry cream in a mixer and blend with the whisk until smooth. Slowly beat in the creamed butter and praline and blend until smooth.

Shelf life: 48 hours, refrigerated, covered, in a non-reactive container.

8. Orange Curd

Juice of 5 oranges
Zest of 2 oranges
30 g (1 oz) cornstarch
60 g (2 oz) egg yolks
200 g (6 1/2 oz) sugar
350 g (12 oz) unsalted butter (creamed)

Bring the orange juice to a boil with the grated zest then pour through a fine-meshed sieve.
Whisk together the egg yolks, sugar, and cornstarch in a bowl.
Whisk in the hot orange juice, then transfer to a non-reactive saucepan and cook over medium heat until the mixture simmers then cook for 2 minutes longer.
Transfer to a shallow dish to cool rapidly.
Whisk the creamed butter into the cooled mixture.

Shelf life: 48 hours, refrigerated, covered in a non-reactive container.

9. Light Orange Pastry Cream

125 ml (1 cup) whole milk
125 ml (1 cup) orange juice
Grated orange zest
2 egg yolks
100 g (1/2 cup) sugar
40 g (1 1/3 oz) cornstarch
500 ml (2 cups) whipping cream

Bring the milk to a boil with the zest. Mix the orange juice, yolks, sugar and poudre. Pour the hot milk through a sieve into the egg mixture, mix to blend, return to the heat and simmer until the pastry cream thickens. Transfer to a shallow dish to cool rapidly.
Beat the cool pastry cream until smooth. Beat the whipping cream to soft peaks and fold into the pastry cream.

Shelf life: 24 hours, refrigerated, covered in a non-reactive container.

10. Light Vanilla Pastry Cream

500 g (1 lb) vanilla pastry cream
250 ml (1 cup) whipping cream

Beat the cold pastry cream in a mixer until smooth. Beat the whipping cream to soft peaks and fold into the pastry cream.

Shelf life: 24 hours, refrigerated, covered in a non-reactive container.

11. Light Pistachio Cream

500 g (1 lb) pastry cream
200 g (6 1/2 oz) pistachio butter
500 ml (2 cups) whipping cream

Beat the pastry cream and pistachio butter (peeled pistachios, puréed with sugar) together until smooth. Beat the whipping cream to soft peaks and fold into the pastry cream.

Shelf life: 24 hours, refrigerated, covered in a non-reactive container'

12. Walnut Buttercream

500 g (1 lb) buttercream
200 g. (6 1/2 oz) walnut paste
200 g (6 1/2 oz) walnut brittle

Blend together the buttercream and walnut paste. Chop the walnut brittle ("nougatine") finely and stir into the buttercream.

Shelf life: 1 week, refrigerated, covered in a non-reactive container.

13. "Duguesclin" Cream

250 g (8 oz) powdered sugar
250 g (8 oz) powdered almonds
220 g (7 oz) unsalted butter, creamed
500 g (1 lb) pastry cream

Mix the creamed butter, powdered sugar and powdered almonds until smooth.
Whisk the cold pastry cream into the almond mixture and blend until smooth.
Use right away or refrigerate.

Shelf life: 48 hours, refrigerated, covered, in a non-reactive container.

14. Chiboust

500 ml (2 cups) milk
8 egg yolks
100 g (3 1/2 oz) sugar
50 g (1 2/3 oz) cornstarch
1/2 vanilla bean
4 leaves or 2 pkg (2 tsps) unflavored gelatin, softened
8 egg whites
200 g sugar + 65 ml (2 fl oz) water
(cooked to hard ball stage (120 C (248 F))

Make a vanilla pastry cream with the milk, egg yolks, sugar, vanilla bean and cornstarch.
Simultaneously, make an Italian meringue with the egg whites, whipped to soft peaks and the sugar syrup.

Add the softened gelatin to the hot pastry cream then fold the warm meringue into the warm pastry cream.
Use as a filling right away.

Shelf life: 12 hours

15. Crème Brulée with Black Currants

250 ml (1 cup) whole milk
250 ml (1 cup) light or heavy ceam
4 egg yolks
60 g (2 oz) sugar
20 ml (2/3 fl oz) black currrant liqueur
1/2 vanilla bean, split and scraped

Bring the milk to a boil with the vanilla bean, add the cream and return to a boil, remove the vanilla bean.
Whisk together the yolks and sugar until light, whisk the hot milk into the egg mixture, then add the liqueur.
Pour the custard into shallow ovenproof dishes and cook at 120 C (250 F) about 20 minutes. Cool before caramelizing the top.

16. Crème Caramel

200 g (6 1/2 oz) sugar
60 ml (2 fl oz) water
1 L (1 qt) whole milk
6 large eggs
200 g (6 1/2 oz) sugar
1/2 vanilla bean, split, scraped

Cook the sugar and water in a heavy saucepan until it becomes a dark golden caramel. Pour into individual soufflé dishes and swirl to coat the sides and bottom.
Bring the milk to a boil with the vanilla bean. Whisk the eggs and sugar until light. Pour the hot milk over the egg mixture, stir to blend then pour the custard into the dishes coated with caramel.
Place in a water bath and cook at 180 C (350 F) about 30 minutes or until set. Cool before serving.

17. Bavarian Cream

Make a crème anglaise with the milk, sugar and egg yolks.
Off the heat, stir in the gelatin (softened) and flavoring then pour through a sieve and chill, stirring occasionally.
Whip the cream to soft peaks in a cold bowl. When the custard begins to set, fold in the whipped cream and mold immediately.

Bavarian Cream	Milk	Sugar Yolks	Egg	Gelatin	Flavoring	Cream	Special Instructions
Vanilla	1 l (1 qt)	500 g (1 lb)	15	15 g (1 tbl)	1 vanilla bean	1 l (1 qt)	Infuse the vanilla bean (split, scraped) into the milk
Orange	500 m (2 cups)	300 g (10 oz)	10	8 g (1/2 tbl)	6 oranges (juice and zest)	1 l (1 qt)	Infuse the zest into the milk, whisk the juice into egg yolks and sugar
Chestnut	500 ml (2 cups)	50 g (1 2/3 oz)	8	8 g (1/2 tbl)	500 g (1 lb) sweetened chestnut purée + 40 ml (3 scant tbls) rum	1 l (1 qt)	Blend the chestnut purée into the cooked custard until smooth
Coffee	1 l (1 qt)	500 g (1 lb)	15	15 g (1 tbl)	70 ml (2,3 fl oz) coffee flavoring	1 l (1 qt)	
Pistachio	1 l (1 qt)	500 g (1 lb)	15	15 g (1 tbl)	250 (8 oz) pureed pistachios	1 l (1 qt)	Blend the puréed pistachios into the cooked custard until smooth
Maraschino	1 l (1 qt)	500 g (1 lb)	15	15 (1 tbl)	160 ml (5 fl oz) maraschino syrup	1 l	
Tea	1 l (1 qt)	500 g (1 lb)	15	15 g (1 tbl)	16 tea bags	1 l (1 qt)	Infuse tea into milk for 15 minutes before making the custard
Mint	1 l (1 qt)	400 g (14 oz)	15	15 g (1 tbl)	30 g (1 oz) fresh mint leaves + 200 g mint syrup		Infuse the mint leaves into the milk, add the syrup
Walnut	1 l (1 qt)	500 g (1 lb)	15	15 g (1 tbl)	240 g puréed walnuts	1 l (1 qt)	**Liquid Caramel:** cook 380 g (13 oz) sugar (dissolved in water) to a golden caramel, add 120 ml (scant 1/2 cup) and stir to dissolve. Add the liquid caramel to the hot milk before mixing the custard.
Caramel	1 l (1 qt)	80 g (2 2/3 oz)	15	15 g (1 tbl)	500 g liquid caramel	1 l (1 qt)	

1. Ganache

250 ml (1 cup) whole milk
250 ml (1 cup) heavy cream
750 g (1 1/2 lbs) bittersweet chocolate
50 g (1 2/3 oz) glucose
Chop the chocolate and bring the milk, cream and glucose to a boil. Off the heat, add the chocolate to the hot milk and whisk until smooth. Transfer to a shallow dish to cool. Stir the firm ganache to a spreadable consistency before using.

Shelf life: one week, refrigerated, in a non-reactive container.

2. Orange Ganache

125 ml (1/2 cup) whole milk
125 ml (1/2 cup) heavy cream
250 ml (1 cup) orange juice
750 g (1 1/2 lbs) bittersweet chocolate
50 g (1 2/3 oz) glucose

Same technique as first ganache (bring milk, cream and juice to a boil together).

Shelf life: one week, refrigerated in a non-reactive container.

3. Ganache for Tarts

250 ml (1 cup) heavy cream
25 g (3/4 oz) glucose
200 g (6 1/2 oz) bittersweet chocolate
50 g (1 2/3 oz) unsalted butter, creamed

Same technique as the first ganache. Whisk in the butter at the end.
Pour into tart shells while still liquid and chill to set.

4. Licorice Ganache for Tarts

250 ml (1 cup) heavy cream
25 g (3/4 oz) glucose
200 g (6 1/2 oz bittersweet chocolate
10 g (1/3 oz) licorice powder
50 g (1 2/3 oz) unsalted butter (creamed)
Mix the licorice powder into the cream, bring to a boil. Same technique as plain ganache for tarts.

III - Mousses

1. Hazelnut Mousse

500 g (1 lb) unsalted butter
250 g (8 oz) hazelnut butter
500 g (1 lb) Italian meringue

Cream the butter.
Add the unsweetened hazelnut butter and stir until smooth.
Gently fold in the Italian meringue.
Use as a filling right away (see "Nut Lovers' Dream").

Shelf life: 48 hours, refrigerated, in a covered non-reactive container

2. Chocolate Mousse

250 g (8 oz) bittersweet chocolate
400 ml whipping cream
200 g (6 1/2 oz) bombe mixture

Melt the chocolate over a water bath.
Whip the cream to soft peaks in a cold bowl.
Fold in 1/2 of the cream into the chocolate to lighten it.
Fold in the remaining whipped cream and the bombe mixture then stir very gently until completely mixed in.
Use as a filling right away.

Shelf life: 48 hours, refrigerated, in a covered non-reactive container

3. Lemon Mousse

8 egg yolks
160 g (5 1/2 oz) sugar
200 ml (7 fl oz) whole milk
240 ml (8 fl oz) lemon juice
1/2 tbl unflavored gelatin, softened

200 g (6 1/2 oz) Italian meringue
100 ml (3.5 ml) whipping cream

Whisk the yolks and the sugar together until light.
Bring the milk and lemon juice to a boil. Whisk the hot liquid into the egg yolks, then cook over a very low heat, stirring constantly, until the

mixture coats the spoon.
Off the heat, stir in the softened gelatin. Pour through a fine-meshed strainer. Refrigerate and stir occasionally to cool it quickly.
When it thickens, but the gelatin is not set, fold in the meringue and cream, whipped to soft peaks.
Use as a filling right away and set the mixture in the freezer.

4. Fresh Cheese Mousse

150 g (5 oz) sugar
40 ml (3 tbls) water
3 egg yolks
1/2 tbl gelatin, softened
400 ml (14 fl oz) whipping cream
600 g (1 lb 3 1/2 oz) ricotta, drained
1 tsp vanilla extract
Drain the ricotta in a coffee filter or cheesecloth about 1 hour or until the cheese is slightly firm.
Cook the sugar and water to 118 C (240 F).
Whisk the yolks until light. Whisk the hot sugar syrup into the egg yolks, add the softened gelatin and beat until very foamy and the mixture is cool.
Whip the cream to soft peaks. Stir the drained ricotta, whipped cream and vanilla into the egg yolks.
Use as a filling right away and place in freezer to set quickly.

5. Fruit Mousse

500 g (1 lb) fruit purée (raspberries, black currants, pears, apples, mango, kiwi, coconut, apricot, passion fruit, blackberries or red currants)
12 oz (scant tbl) gelatin, softened
300 ml (10 fl oz) whipping cream
250 g (8 oz) Italian meringue
Bring 1/2 of the fruit juice to a boil and stir in the softened gelatin.
Stir in the remaining juice and pour through a sieve.
Whip the cream to soft peaks and gently fold into the fruit purée along with the Italian meringue.
Use as a filling right away and place in the freezer to set quickly.

IV - Various Mixtures

1. Italian Meringue

200 g (7 oz) egg whites
400 g (14 oz) sugar
130 ml (4 fl oz) water
Beat the egg whites to soft peaks.
Meanwhile, cook the sugar and water to the hard ball stage (120 C (248 F)).
With the mixer on medium speed, pour the hot sugar syrup slowly into the egg whites and continue to beat at high speed until the mixture is cool.

Shelf life: 24 hours, refrigerated, in a covered, non-reactive container.

Which Meringue to Use?

Italian Meringue, is used as an ingredient in fillings and on its own as a decoration. It is primarily used to lighten mousses of all kinds and is a sort of icing when piped in a decorative design on cakes such as "bûches" and used as a topping on tarts.

French Meringue and Swiss Meringue are baked until crispy and used as a base or layer in combination with fillings and fruits in such desserts as "vacherin" and "succés". They are grouped with the cakes because they are also used in layered desserts.

2. Bombe mixture

250 g (8 oz) egg yolks
300 g (10 oz) sugar
100 ml (3.5 fl oz) water

Beat the eggs until light in the mixer.
Meanwhile, cook the sugar and water to (118 C (240 F)).
With the mixer on medium speed, slowly pour the hot syrup into the egg yolks, continue to beat at high speed until the mixture is cool.

Shelf life: Store in a covered, non-reactive container in the freezer.

3. Gratin Mixture

500 g (1 lb) bombe mixture
250 ml (1 cup) whipping cream

Whip the cream to soft peaks and fold into the bombe mixture.
Spoon this mixture over the food that is be gratinéed.

4. Blanc Manger Mixture

250 ml (1 cup) whole milk
50 g (1 2/3 oz) sugar
1/2 vanilla bean
80 g (2 2/3 oz) blanched almonds
1 tsp gelatin, softened
150 ml (5 fl oz) whipping cream

Bring the milk to a boil with the sugar, vanilla bean, and almonds. Infuse 20 minutes then purée in the food processor.
Return to the pan, bring to a simmer and stir in the softened gelatin.
Cool until the mixture begins to set then fold in lightly whipped cream. Mold immediately and set in the freezer.

5. "Far Breton" Mixture

7 large eggs
350 g (12 oz) sugar
300 g (10 oz) flour
1 L (1 qt) whole milk
20 ml (1 1/2 tbls) Armagnac

Whisk together the eggs and sugar.
Stir in the flour.
Whisk in the milk and Armagnac a little at a time and blend until smooth.
Transfer to the prepared baking dish and cook immediately.

V - Les préparations glacées

1. Frozen Nougat Créole

150 g (5 oz) egg whites
200 g (6 1/2 oz) honey
80 g (scant 3 oz) glucose
80 g (scant 3 oz) sugar
900 ml (scant 1 qt) whipping cream
300 g (10 oz) rum-macerated raisins
200 g (6 1/2 oz) crumbled nougatine

Cook the sugar, honey and glucose to 125 C (250 F).
Meanwhile beat the egg whites to soft peaks. With the mixer running, pour the hot syrup into the egg whites and beat until the mixture is thick and cool.
Whip the cream to soft peaks and carefully fold into the cooled meringue. Fold in the rasins and nougatine.
Transfer the mixture to a mold and place in the freezer until firm.

2. Mint Granité

500 ml (2 cups) water
30 fresh mint leaves
250 ml (1 cup) simple syrup
2 drops mint oil

Bring the water to a boil with the mint leaves. cover, remove from the heat and infuse 15 minutes. Stir in the syrup and mint oil.
Pour through a sieve into a shallow dish.
Cover and place in the freezer several hours.
Once the granité is frozen, it can be portioned by scraping the surface with a spoon to obtain icy chunks. Serve immediately.

3. Frozen Coconut Mousse

125 ml (1 cup) puréed coconut
125 ml (1 cup) heavy syrup (2/3 sugar, 1/3 water)
500 ml (2 cups) whipping cream

Mix the syrup and coconut. Whip the cream to stiff peaks and fold into the coconut mixture. Transfer to the mold, cover and place in the freezer several hours.

4. Frozen Tea Mousse

125 ml (1 cup) whole milk
250 g (8 oz) sugar
8 egg yolks
12 g (1/3 oz) tea leaves
125 ml (1 cup) whipping cream

Heat the milk and infuse the tea 15 minutes.
Pour the milk through a fine-meshed sieve and

make a crème anglaise with the milk, egg yolks and sugar.
Cool the mixture quickly (in an ice bath). Whip the cream to soft peaks and fold in the crème anglaise. Transfer to the mold, cover and place in the freezer several hours.

5. Frozen "Parfait" (rum, Armagnac, licorice and Créole)

8 egg yolks
125 ml (1 cup) simple syrup
125 ml (1 cup) heavy cream

Combine the egg yolks and syrup in a non-reactive bowl. Set over a water bath and whisk until the mixture is thick and lemon-colored. Remove from the heat and beat until the mixture is cool. Whisk in the flavoring (see below). Whip the cream to soft peaks and fold in the egg mixture. Transfer to the mold, cover and freeze several hours.

Créole:
150 g (5 oz) rum-macerated rasins

Armagnac:
80 ml (2 2/3 fl oz) Armagnac

Rum:
80 ml (2 2/3 fl oz) rum

Licorice:
20 g (2/3 oz) licorice powder
5 g 1/16 fl oz licorice extract

6. Ice Cream (made with eggs) (vanilla, coffee, praline, chestnut, caramel)

Bring the milk to a boil with half the sugar and unsalted butter.
Whisk together the egg yolks, remaining sugar and trimoline.
Whisk the hot milk into the beated eggs, return to the pan, bring the mixture to 85 C (150 F) and cook, stirring constantly for 2-3 minutes or until the mixture coats the back of a spoon.
Pour through a fine-meshed sieve and cool quickly in an ice bath.
Churn in an ice cream maker and store in the freezer.

Ice Cream	Milk + + unsalted butter	Sugar	Trimoline	Egg yolks	Flavoring
Vanilla	1 l (1 qt) + 50 g (1 2/3 oz)	250 g (8 oz)	50 g (2 2/3 oz)	7	1 vanilla bean
Coffee	1 l (1 qt) + 50 g (2 2/3 oz)	250 g (8 oz)	50 g (2 2/3 oz)	7	30 ml (1 fl oz) coffee syrup
Praline	1 l (1 qt) + 50 g (2 2/3 oz)	125 g (4 oz)	50 g (2 2/3 oz)	7	250 g (8 oz) praline paste
Chestnut	1 l (1 qt) + 50 g (2 2/3 oz)	250 g (8 oz)	50 g (2 2/3 oz)	7	300 g chestnut purée
Caramel	1 l (1 qt) + 50 g (2 2/3 oz)	125 g (4 oz)	50 g (2 2/3 oz)	7	250 g (8 oz) caramel*
Walnut	1 l (1 qt) + 50 g (2 2/3 oz)	230 g (7 1/3 oz)	50 g (2 2/3 oz)	7	100 g (3 1/2 oz) puréedwalnuts
Hazelnut	1 l (1 qt) + 50 g (2 2/3 oz)	250 g (8 oz)	50 g (2 2/3 oz)	7	200 g (6 1/2 oz) puréed hazelnut

*Caramel : Cook 250 g (8 oz) sugar (dry) to a caramel, dissolve with the cooked mixture.
Note: Ice cream made with egg yolks does not contain a stabilizer because the shelf life is just a few days to a week. It is important to date each container and rotate the stock.

7. Sorbets (coconut, mango, passion fruit, Granny Smith)

Make the heavy syrup in a non-reactive saucepan. Combine 1 L (1 qt) water, 1.2 kg (2 lbs 8 oz) sugar, and 120 g (scant 4 oz) glucose, bring to a simmer and cook 1-2 minutes to completely dissolve the sugar. Cool completely. Combine the amounts of syrup and fruit purée called for in the formulas that follow. Note that it is recommended to weigh the ingredients
Pour through a fine-meshed sieve and churn in an ice cream freezer.
Transfer to a covered container and store in the freezer.

Flavor	Syrup	Fruit purée
Coconut	1 kg (2.2 lbs)	1 kg (2.2 lbs)
Mango	1 kg (2.2 lbs)	1 kg (2.2 lbs)
Passion fruit	1.3 kg (2.9 lbs)	700 g (1.5 lbs)
Granny Smith	1 kg (2.2 lbs)	1 kg (2.2 lbs)

VI - Les sauces d'accompagnement

1. Fruit coulis

Make a simple syrup by combining 1 L (1 qt) water and 1.2 kg (2.5 lbs) sugar and bring to a boil to dissolve the sugar.
Measure the syrup, fruit purée and liqueur according to the following formulas, combine and pour through a fine-meshed sieve. .

Shelf life: one week, refrigerated, in a covered, non-reactive container.

Flavor	Syrup	Fruit purée	Liqueur (or water)
Black currant	250 g (8 oz)	500 g (1 lb)	50 ml (4 tbls) black currant liqueur
Raspberry	250 g (8 oz)	500g (1 lb)	50 ml (4 tbls) raspberry liqueur
Blackberry	250 g (8 oz)	500 g (1 lb)	50 ml (4 tbls) blackberry liqueur
Abricot	250 g (8 oz)	500 g (1 lb)	
Pears	125 g (4 oz)	500 g (1 lb)	50 ml (4 tbls) pear alcool
Mango	250 g (8 oz)	500 g (1 lb)	
Kiwi	250 g (8 oz)	500 g (1 lb)	
Prune	400 g (14 oz)	500 g (1 lb)	250 ml (1 cup) boiling water
Red currant	250 g (8 oz)	500 g (1 lb)	

2. Crème Anglaise (vanilla, coffee, pistachio, cinnamon)

1 L (1 qt) whole milk
12 egg yolks
300 g (10 oz) sugar
200 ml (7 fl oz) heavy cream
Flavoring
Whisk the egg yolks with half the sugar until light.
Bring the milk to a boil with the remaining sugar and whisk into the egg yolks. Return the mixture to the saucepan and cook the mixture at 85 C (150 F) 2-3 minutes until the custard coats a spoon. Pour through a fine-meshed sieve and cool quickly in an ice bath.
Whisk the cream to very soft peaks and stir into the custard.
Shelf life: 24 hours, refrigerated in a covered, non-reactive container.

Vanilla: Split the vanilla bean, scrape the seeds and infuse into the milk.

Coffee: 40 ml (3 1/2 tbl) coffee syrup added to the cooked custard.
Pistachio: 140 g (4 3/4 oz) puréed pistachios, added to the cooked custard.
Cinnamon: 40 g (1 1/3 oz) cinnamon sticks, infused into the milk.

3. Sabayon (rum, raspberry "eau de vie", Grand Marnier, kirsch, Muscat, Calvados)

8 egg yolks
160 g (5 1/3 oz) sugar
80 ml (2.5 fl oz) liqueur
100 ml (3.5 fl oz) heavy cream
Whisk the egg yolks and sugar together over a water bath until the mixtures reaches 45 C (112 F) and is thick and lemon-colored.
Remove from the heat and beat the mixture as it cools, adding the liqueur a little at a time.
When the mixture is cool, fold in lightly whipped cream.
Shelf life: use immediately.

4. Caramel Sauces

100 g (3 1/2 oz) glucose
300 g (10 oz) sugar
Liquid for deglazing
(see flavorings below)
Melt the glucose in an all-copper sugar pot. Add the sugar a little at a time and stir as the mixture cooks to a light brown caramel.

Warm the deglazing liquid and stir into the caramel.
Return to the heat and bring to a simmer, stirring to combine.
Pour through a fine-meshed sieve.
Shelf life: one week, refrigerated, in a covered, non-reactive container.

Deglazing Liquids for Caramel Sauces	
Caramel	300 ml (10 fl oz) water + juice of 1 lemon
Tea	300 ml (10 fl oz) + juice of 1 lemon
Orange	350 ml (12 fl oz) orange juice
Raspberry	250 g (8 oz) seedless raspberry purée + 100 ml (3.5 fl oz) water
Black currant	200 g (6 1/2 oz) black currant purée + 200 ml (7 fl oz) water
Apricot	300 g (10 oz) apricot purée + 200 ml (7 fl oz) water
Hazelnut	400 g puréed hazelnuts + 100 ml (3.5 fl oz) water

5. Various Sauces

Coconut Sauce
200 g (6 1/2 oz) fresh puréed coconut
100 g (3 1/2 oz) powdered sugar
Juice of 1 lemon
Blend all the ingredients in a food processor until smooth.
Shelf life: 48 hours, refrigerated, in a covered, non-reactive container.

Cherry Sauce
200 g (6 1/2 oz) fresh pitted cherries
40 g (1 1/3 oz) powdered sugar
20 g (2/3 oz) marascino syrup
Blend all the ingredients in a food processor until smooth.
Shelf life: 24 hours, refrigerated in a covered, non-reactive container.

Passion Fruit Sauce
4 passion fruits
50 g (1 2/3 oz) syrup
25 g (scant oz) powdered sugar

Scoop out the center of the fruits and blend in a food processor with the syrup and sugar until smooth.
Shelf life: 24 hours, refrigerated, in a covered, non-reactive container.

Chocolate Sauce
250 ml (1 cup) whole milk
250 g (8 oz) bittersweet chocolate
80 g (2 2/3 oz) heavy cream
40 g (1 1/3 oz) unsalted butter

Bring the milk to a boil. Chop the chocolate and add to the milk and whisk until the mixture is smooth.
Off the heat, stir in the cream and butter and blend until smooth.
Keep the sauce warm in a water bath until ready to serve.

Shelf life: 24 hours, refrigerated, in a covered, non-reactive container.

VII - Pastries

1. Sweet Pie Pastry

250 g (8 oz) unsalted butter
250 g (8 oz) powdered sugar
100 g (3 1/2 oz) whole eggs
500 g (1 lb) unbleached flour
1/2 tsp vanilla extract

Cream the butter and powdered sugar until smooth. Stir in the eggs one at a time. Mix in the vanilla and flour, stirring until the dough is just mixed, don't overwork.

Transfer the dough to a sheet of plastic wrap, cover, form into a disk and refrigerate until firm.

Yield: 30 8 cm (3 in) circles (used to line 6 cm (2 3/4 in) tart molds).

2. Hazelnut Pie Pastry

300 g (10 oz) unsalted butter
200 g (6 1/2 oz) powdered sugar
120 g (scant 4 oz) eggs
50 g (1 2/3 oz) powdered hazelnuts
500 g (1 lb) unbleached flour
2 g (scant 1/2 tsp) salt
1/2 tsp vanilla extract

Mix the powdered nuts with the flour.
Procedure is the same as sweet pie pastry.
Same yield as sweet pie pastry

3. Puff Pastry

500 g (1 lb) unbleached flour
12 g (2 tsp) salt
125 g (4 oz) unsalted butter, melted
250 ml (1 cup) cold water
250 g (8 oz) unsalted butter, chilled

Make a dough with the flour, salt, melted butter and water. Knead a little until the dough is smooth but don't over work.

Cover and refrigerate the dough 30 minutes. Pound the cold butter with a rolling pin to make it pliable and form into a square.

Roll the dough into a small circle, place the square of butter in the center and fold the edges to cover the butter and seal like an envelope. Roll out into a long rectangle and fold into thirds. Turn the dough a quarter turn and repeat the rolling and folding process. Cover and let the dough rest in the refrigerator 30 minutes. Make 5 "turns" in all, allowing the dough to rest again after the 4th and 5th turn. Roll out and cut into desired shapes.

Yield: 18 circles (2 mm (1/12 in thick), 13 cm (5 in) diameter
36 rectangles (1 mm (1 /20 in thick) 10 cm X 4 cm (4 in X 1 1/2 in)

4. Baba Dough

(Yield: 36 individual babas or savarins)
500 g (1 lb) unbleached flour
10 g (2 tsp) salt
25 g (scant 1 oz) fresh yeast
5 large eggs
200 g (6 1/2 unsalted butter, melted
100 g (3 1/2 oz) raisins, macerated in rum

Dissolve the yeast in a little warm water with a pinch of sugar.

Combine all the ingredients, except the butter, in a mixer and blend at medium speed until the dough is smooth, elastic and pulls away from the sides of the bowl.

Scrape down the sides, cover and let rise at room temperature about 1 hour or until doubled. Deflate the dough, return to the mixer and on low speed blend in the melted butter. When the dough is smooth and pulling away from the sides, add the raisins.

Fill the buttered molds halfway with dough (most easily done by pinching off small handfuls of dough). Cover and let rise about 30 minutes. Bake in a preheated 210 C (415 F) oven until puffed and golden, about 15-20 minutes.

Simple Syrup
1 L (1 qt) water
500 (1 lb) sugar

Combine the water and sugar, bring to a boil. Add wine or liqueur to flavor and cool.

Soak the babas while still hot from the oven in the syrup until they have absorbed syrup through to the center of the cakes. Transfer to a rack to drain excess syrup and cool.

5. Cream Puff Dough

(Yield: 25 "salambos" or 80 "profiteroles")
125 ml (1 cup) whole milk
125 ml (1 cup) water
100 g (3 1/2 oz) unsalted butter
5 g (1 tsp) salt
4 large eggs
150 g (5 oz) unbleached flour

Bring the milk, water, butter and salt to a boil. Off the heat, add the flour all at once and stir

VIII - Cakes and Baked Meringues

1. Sponge cake

(Yield: 1 sheet 40 X 60 cm (16 X 24 in))
250 g (8 oz) eggs
75 g (2 1/2 oz) egg yolks
110 g (3 2/3 oz) sugar
110 g (3 2/3 oz) unbleached flour

Whisk the eggs, egg yolks and sugar over a water bath in the bowl of the mixer. When the mixture is warm (50 C (122 F)), beat at high speed until thick and cool.

Sift the flour over the egg mixture and gently fold in.

Transfer the mixture to a baking sheet lined with parchment paper and bake at 230 C (450 F) for 10 minutes.

2. Chocolate sponge cake

(Yield: 1 sheet 40 X 60 cm (16 X 24 in))
110 g (3 2/3 oz) egg yolks
120 g (3 3/4 oz) sugar
200 g (6 1/2 oz) egg whites
40 g (1 1/3 oz) sugar
60 g (2 oz) cornstarch
60 g (2 oz) unbleached flour
30 g 1 oz) cocoa powder

Beat the yolks with 120 g sugar until thick and lemon colored. Beat the egg whites to stiff peaks then whisk in 40 g sugar.

Sift the cornstarch, flour and cocoa powder together. Sift this mixture over the beaten egg yolks and fold in. Lastly, fold in the beaten egg whites.

Transfer to a baking sheet lined with parchment paper and bake at 220 C (425 F) for 10 minutes.

3. Almond Sponge Cake

(Yield: 1 sheet 40 X 60 cm (16 X 24 in))
125 g (4 oz) sugar
125 g (4 oz) powdered almonds

---

to combine. Return to low heat and dry the mixture a little. Off the heat, beat in the eggs one at a time, stirring well after each addtion.

Pipe out the mixture in the desired shape and size (the dough will not keep unbaked). Brush the formed pastries with egg glaze, smooth the top with the back of a fork and bake in a preheated 220 C (425 F) oven until puffed and golden, about 15-20 minutes.

180 g (6 oz) eggs
120 g (3 3/4 oz) egg whites
20 g (2/3 oz) sugar
35 g (1 1/16 oz) unbleached flour
25 g (scant 1 oz) unsalted butter, melted

Beat the eggs, 125 g sugar and almonds until thick and light.

Beat the egg whites to stiff peaks and whisk in 20 g sugar.

Sift the flour over the egg yolk mixture and fold in.

Gently fold in the beaten egg whites and melted butter.

Transfer to a baking sheet lined with parchment paper and bake at 230 C (450 F) for 10-11 minutes.

4. Ladyfingers

(Yield: 1 sheet 40 X 60 cm (16 X 24 in))
6 eggs, separated
150 g (5 oz) sugar
75 g (2 1/2 oz) unbleached flour
75 g (2 1/2 oz) cornstarch

In a mixer at high speed, beat the egg whites and sugar to a thick, smooth meringue.

Gently stir in the egg yolks.

Sift the cornstarch and flour over the egg mixture and gently fold in.

Line a baking sheet with parchment paper. Using a medium-size plain tip, pipe the mixture in strips on the baking sheet.

Bake at 220 C (425 F) for 12 minutes.

5. "Russe"

(Yield: 1 sheet 40 X 60 cm (16 X 24 in))
300 g (10 oz) sugar
180 g (6 oz) powdered almonds
450 g (15 2/3 oz) egg whites

Mix together 170 g (5 2/3 oz) sugar, 100 g (3 1/2 oz) egg whites and the powdered almonds.

Beat the remaining egg whites to stiff peaks and whisk in the remaining sugar.

Fold the beaten egg whites into the almond mixture.

Transfer to a baking sheet lined with parchment paper and bake at 175 C (350 F) 20-25 minutes.

VIII - Cakes and Baked Meringues *(end)*

6. Orange Sponge Cake

(Yield: 1 sheet 40 X 60 cm (16 X 24 in))

20 g (2/3 oz) candied orange peel, chopped
200 g (6 1/2 oz) almond paste
100 g (3 1/2 oz) egg yolks
80 g (2 2/3 oz) unbleached flour
60 g (2 oz) cornstarch
170 g (5 2/3 oz) egg whites
80 g (2 2/3 oz) sugar

Blend the almond paste, egg yolks and orange peel with the paddle of the mixer. Sift together the cornstarch and flour and gently fold into the first mixture.
Whip the egg whites to stiff peaks and whisk in the sugar.
Transfer to a baking sheet lined with parchment paper and bake at 220 C (425 F) for 12 minutes.

7. Coconut Sponge Cake

(Yield: 1 sheet 40 X 60 cm (16 X 24 in))

190 g (6 1/3 oz) sugar
90 g (3 oz) powdered almonds
100 g (3 1/2 oz) freshly grated coconut
270 g (8 2/3 oz) eggs
180 g (6 oz) egg whites
30 g (1 oz) sugar
50 g (1 2/3 oz) unbleached flour
40 g (1 1/3 oz) unsalted butter, melted

In the mixer, whisk together the eggs, 190 g sugar, the almonds and coconut until thick and light.
Beat the egg whites to stiff peaks and whisk in the 30 g sugar.
Sift the flour over the whole egg mixture and gently fold in.
Fold in the beaten egg whites and melted butter.
Transfer to a baking sheet lined with parchment paper and bake at 220 C (425 F) for 12 minutes.

8. Hazelnut or Coconut Meringue ("Dacquoise")

(Yield: 1 sheet 40 X 60 cm (16 X 24 in)
or 45 small circles for individual desserts)

165 g (5 1/2 oz) sugar
165 g (5 1/2 oz) powdered hazelnuts*
40 g (1 1/3 oz) unbleached flour
250 g (8 oz) egg whites
180 g (6 oz) sugar
*For the coconut meringue, replace the nuts with an equal amount of freshly grated coconut.

Mix together the 165 g sugar, powdered nuts and flour.
Beat the egg whites and 180 g sugar to a firm and glossy meringue.
Fold in the nut mixture and transfer to a baking sheet lined with parchment paper. Bake at 200 C (400 F) for 20 minutes.

9. Almond Meringue ("Succés")

(Yield: 7 20 cm (8 in) rounds or
48 small rounds for individual desserts)

250 g (8 oz) powdered almonds
50 g (1 2/3 oz) unbleached flour
300 g (10 oz) sugar
300 g (10 oz) egg whites

Mix together the powdered almonds, 100 g (3 1/2 oz) sugar and the flour.
Beat the egg whites and remaining sugar to a firm, glossy meringue.
Fold in the nut mixture and transfer to a baking sheet lined with parchment paper. Bake at 230 C (450 F) for 12-14 minutes.

10. French Meringue

(Yield: 4 20 cm (8 in) rounds or
24 small rounds for individual desserts)

125 g (4 oz) egg whites
250 g (8 oz) sugar

Beat the egg whites to stiff peaks then whisk in 60 g (2 oz) sugar to "tighten" the meringue and make it firm and glossy.
Gently fold in the remaining sugar. Use a medium plain tip to pipe out the size and shape meringue needed on a baking sheet lined with parchment paper.
Bake at 100 C (200 F) for 2 hours.

IX - Various Mixtures

1. Chocolate Cigarette Batter

40 g (1 1/3 oz) powdered sugar
40 g (1 1/3 oz) egg whites
40 g (1 1/3 oz) unsalted butter, melted
20 g (2/3 oz) unbleached flour
20 g (2/3 oz) cocoa powder

Whisk together the egg whites and powdered sugar then whisk in the melted butter.
Sift the flour and cocoa powder together over the first mixture and stir well to blend.

2. Basic Cigarette Batter

100 g (3 1/2 oz) unsalted butter
100 g (3 1/2 oz) powdered sugar
100 g (3 1/2 oz) egg whites
75 g (2 1/2 oz) unbleached flour
1/2 tsp vanilla extract

Cream the butter and powdered sugar. Stir in the egg whites (room temperature). Stir in the vanilla and flour and blend until smooth.
Cover and let rest 30 minutes before baking. (see "Croustillants")

3. Almond Brittle ("Nougatine")

300 g (10 oz) fondant
200 g (6 1/2 oz) glucose
250 g (8 oz) sliced almonds
(or chopped walnuts)
1 tbl unsalted butter

Melt the glucose, add the fondant and bring to a boil.
Add the nuts and cook over medium heat until the caramel darkens to the desired color.
Stir in the butter and pour onto an oiled marble surface to cool and shape.

Shelf life: 2 weeks in an air tight container in a cool place.

4. Pineapple Filling

200 g (6 1/2 oz) pineapple in heavy syrup
100 g (3 1/2 oz) apricot jam
20 ml (4 tbls) rum

Chop the pineapple very finely and melt the jam. Combine with the rum and stir until blended.

Shelf life: 15 days, refrigerated, in a covered, non-reactive container.

5. "Croustillants"

(see recipes below)
Cream the unsalted butter, stir in the sugar, honey, nuts and liqueur.
When the mixture is smooth, stir in the flour.
Let the mixture rest 30 minutes before forming and baking.
Spread the batter in thin circles on a baking sheet lined with parchment and bake at 200 C (400 F) until brown and crispy.

Shelf life: Store the baked cookies up to 2 weeks in an air-tight container in a cool, dry place.

6. Florentines

100 g (3 1/2 oz) sugar
70 g (2 1/3 oz) honey
70 g (2 1/3 oz) unsalted butter
130 g (4 1/2 oz) heavy cream
100 g (3 1/2 oz) candied orange peel, chopped
170 g (6 1/4 oz) sliced almonds
40 g(1 1/3 oz) candied cherries, chopped
50 g (1 2/3 oz) unbleached flour

Combine the sugar, honey, butter and cream in a heavy saucepan and cook to 105 C (210 F).
Off the heat, stir in the candied fruits, almonds and flour.
Same baking procedure as "croustillants".
Shelf life: same as "croustillants.

"Croustillants"

(Recipes)

	Almond	Walnut	Pistachio	Raspberry
Unsalted butter	100 g (31/2 oz)	100 g (31/2 oz)	100 g (31/2 oz)	100 g (31/2 oz)
Sugar	180 g (6 oz)	180 g (6 oz)	180 g (6 oz)	180 g (6 oz)
Honey	20 g (2/3 oz)	20 g (2/3 oz)	20 g (2/3 oz)	20 g (2/3 oz)
Nuts	200 g (61/2 oz)	200 g (61/2 oz)	200 g (61/2 oz)	200 g (61/2 oz)
Fruit juice	100 ml (3.5 fl oz) orange juice	100 ml (3.5 fl oz) orange juice	100 ml (3.5 fl oz) orange juice	100 ml (31/2 oz) raspberry liqueur
Liqueur	50 ml (4 tbls) Kirsch	50 ml (4 tbls) Kirsch	50 ml (4 tbls) Kirsch	50 ml (4 tbls) raspberry liqueur
Flour	50 g (1 2/3 oz)	50 g (12/3 oz)	50 g (12/3 oz)	50 g (12/3 oz)

7. Jelly Glaze

Note: In France "nappage blond" is widely available. It is an apricot-based jelly that melts to a golden glaze. Apricot jam, melted and strained can be substituted. Apple jelly, melted, with nothing added, makes a very good clear glaze and red currant jelly, melted, makes a very good glaze to enhance desserts made with red fruits.

Clear Jelly Glaze
400 g (14 oz) "nappage blond"
150 ml (5 fl oz) pear syrup
100 g (3 1/2 oz) glucose

Red Jelly Glaze
400 g (14 oz) "nappage blond"
150 ml (5 fl oz) black currant liqueur
100 g (3 1/2 oz) glucose

Coffee glaze: Clear jelly glaze + coffee syrup
Green glaze: Clear jelly glaze + green food color
Walnut glaze: Clear jelly glaze + finely chopped walnut brittle

Bring the ingredients to a boil, pour through a fine-meshed sieve.

8. Chocolate Glaze

150 ml (5 fl oz) whole milk
100 ml (3.5 fl oz) water
100 g (3 1/2 oz) sugar
200 g (6 1/2 oz) glucose
300 g (10 oz) fondant
300 g (10 oz) covering chocolate, chopped

Bring the first five ingredients to a boil and stir to blend.
Off the heat, stir in the chopped chocolate. Return to low heat and stir until very smooth and shiny.

Shelf life: 1 week, refrigerated, in a covered, non-reactive container.

9. Pears with Ginger

Syrup (300 g (10 oz) sugar/250 ml (1 cup) water)
10 g (1/3 oz) fresh ginger root, chopped
1 clove
1 pinch freshly ground pepper
4 pears, peeled

Infuse the spices into the syrup. Cut each pear into 12 sections.
Poach the pears in the flavored syrup and cool in the syrup.

Shelf life: 48 hours, refrigerated, in a covered, non-reactive container.

10. Grand Marnier Truffles

500 ml (2 cups) heavy cream*
50 g (1 2/3 oz) glucose
1.1 kg (1 1/4 lbs) bittersweet chocolate, chopped
180 ml (6 fl oz) Grand Marnier

(*Note: Long conservation cream may work better in this recipe whichrequires boiling.)

Bring the cream and glucose to a boil. On low heat, add the chopped chocolate and stir until smooth. Pour into a shallow dish and cool.
Transfer the cool ganache into a bowl and stir in the Grand Marnier. Blend until the mixture is smooth and thick.
Use a large, plain tip to pipe the mixture into bite-size balls.
Refrigerate 1/2 hour to firm, then roll into into smooth balls.
Dip into tempered covering chocolate, cool to set, then coat with cocoa powder.

Shelf life: 2 weeks, refrigerated, in an air tight container.

11. Simple Syrup for Imbibing

1.2 kg (2 1/2 lbs) sugar
1 L (1 qt) water

Bring the water and sugar to a boil. Cool, then stir in the flavoring.

Shelf life: 2 weeks, refrigerated, in a covered, non-reactive container.

Flavoring for 1/2 L (2 cups) Syrup	
Black currant	100 ml (3.5 fl oz) black currant liqueur
Pear	100 ml (3.5 fl oz) pear liqueur
Lemon	400 ml (14 fl oz) lemon juice (strained
Raspberry	100 ml (3.5 fl oz raspberry liqueur
Vanilla	10 ml (2 tsp) vanilla extract
Coffee	15 ml (3 tsp) coffee syrup
Blackberry	100 ml (3.5 fl oz) blackberry liqueur
Cointreau	100 ml (3.5 fl oz) Cointreau
Marascino	100 ml (3.5 fl oz) marascino syrup
Rum	100 ml (3.5 fl oz) rum
Licorice	4 ml (scant 1 tsp) licorice extract
Cocoa	60 g (2 oz) cocoa powder + 250 g ml (1 cup) water
	Bring to a boil, stir to blend

Shelf life: 2 weeks, refrigerated, in a covered, non-reactive container.

Equipment - Important for Good Results

Buying dishes and equipment is an important decision for a restaurant owner or private individual. It is a major investment that warrants serious consideration in order to purchase high quality within your given budget.

1. Dishes

Plates

The appearance of food and the plate it is served on is the first thing that attracts the attention of the diner.

First, it is important the that the colors of the dishes harmonize with the room itself and the linens.

If there there is a logo for the restaurant, the dishes should be in a similar style. The logo, or a monogram in the same script can adorn the plates and give a personalized touch.

As important as the visual effect is, the price and durability of the dishes must be seriously considered. The heavy use in a restaurant can fade the colors of a beautiful plate and some dishes chip more easily than others.

In addition to the basic dishes, it is nice to select a set or two in another pattern (that doesn't clash with the others) in one or two sizes that vary the overall presentation of the meal. The plates for dessert, for example, could be different than the others.

Large plates (10-11 in) are the most versatile and should be purchased in greater numbers. For elaborate presentations, the chef as artist needs a larger "canvas" to arrange foods beautifully without crowding.

However, desserts sometimes look lost on a large presentation plate and the smaller cutlery designed for dessert will look out of proporation.

Goblets

Whether in glass, crystal or another material, one must choose goblets (for serving ice cream and mousse) that are solid as well as elegant.

The rim of the dishes must withstand knocking from silverware, in the dishwasher and stacking in the closet.

Cut glass, although attractive, can chip easily.

Great care must be taken to clean them well so no shards of glass end up in the food.

Acknowledgments

We would like especially to thank M. Bruno Duponchel from St Chomette-Favor, for providing the beautiful plates used in the photographs. The various plates were created by the following manufacturers:

APILCO
ESCHENBACH
LILIEN
PILLIVUYT
VILLEROY AND BOCH
SARREGUEMINES

2. Small Equipment

Knives, Spatulas and more

Choose tools made of stainless steel.

Have off set metal spatulas in several sizes for spreading cake batter in a sheet pan.

Many high quality tools can be found at the hardware store such triangular spatulas (for plaster) and toothed "combs" or "peignes" (for spreading glue).

Pastry chefs have also discovered that the rubber, wood-grained roller used to apply a "faux bois" effect on a painted suface will do the same with chocolate to make a design on sponge cake batter (apply the chocolate, then pour the batter over it).

Pots and Pans

In France, unlined copper pots are used for the cooking of sugar. They conduct heat well and can be spotlessly cleaned with vinegar and coarse salt to insure dependable results with caramelized sugar. The unlined copper pots must not be used for any other purpose as the metal will react with foods, especially eggs. For all other preparations, stainless steel pots with a copper insert in the base are the best.

Cake Molds and Pastry Rings

Molds and pastry rings in different shapes allow French chefs to give a personal touch to their "designer" desserts.

So many shapes and sizes are available that the choice is difficult. For individual desserts, choose small molds that will give a dramatic effect to layered cakes, mousses, and frozen creams. Sturdy, stainless steel molds are the best investment.

Miscellaneous Equipment

a) *Multi-bladed pastry cutter:* Rolling cutting blades attached to a hinged handle to adjust the width. Used for cutting croissants and plaquettes" or rectangles of chocolate.

b) *Spray gun:* Used for spraying chocolate on a dessert (melted with extra coco butter to keep it fluid). A standard paint sprayer with a motor attachment is used, which is warmed to 40 C (98 F) before using.

c) *Chocolate molds:* Use polycarbonate molds which are easy to clean and are not fragile.

d) *Reusable silicon liners:* A non-stick liner for baking sheets which can be used up to 3,000-4,000 times.

e) *"Feuille Guitar":* This French tool spreads an even, paper thin layer of chocolate for leaf-like disks, bark, and fine shavings. it should be cleaned with dry paper towels.

f) *"Rhodoid":* This stiff yet flexible plastic sheet (also available in rolls) was developed in France for making simple chocolate designs. Once the chocolate is firm the plastic is bent slightly to release it.

g) *Plastic chocolate molds:* Usually made in a sheet with a dozen or more designs molded into the plastic. Fill with tempered chocolate and chill until firm.

h) *Edible designs on plastic:* A picture or restaurant logo reproduced in edible coating is pressed onto plastic wrap which is then transferred onto individual desserts.

i) *Parchment paper:* Used to line baking sheets, especially when making sponge cakes. When used under tarts or cookies, the sheets can be reused several times. Parchment sheets with a special coating are used for working with cooked sugar.

Additional Information and Advice

Fruits used for the various decoration

(refer to section «Decorating with fruit»)

Fresh fruits	Fruits in syrup
Strawberries	Pineapple
Raspberries	Apricots
Red currants	Cherries (Amaréna)
Blackberries	Mini pears
Black currants	Mini apples
Apples	
Pears	**Dried fruits**
Peaches	
Grapes	Prunes
Lemons	Raisins
Oranges	
Kiwis	
Star fruit	**Nuts**
Mangoes	
Passion fruit	Pistachios
Gooseberries	Almonds
Bananas	Hazelnuts
	Walnuts

Additional information for decoration with cake, cookies and other mixtures (p. 34-35)

Decorating with cakes and cookies

(Croustillants and Florentines, p. 31)

Ingredients for various Florentines

	Almonds	Walnuts	Pistachios	Raspberries
Butter	100 g (3 1/2 oz)	100 g (3 1/2 oz)	100 g (3 1/2 oz)	100 g (3 1/2 oz)
Sugar	180 g (6 oz)	180 g (6 oz)	180 g (6 oz)	180 g (6 oz)
Honey	20 g (2/3 oz)	20 g (2/3 oz)	20 g (2/3 oz)	20 g (2/3 oz)
Nuts	200 g (7 oz) chopped almonds	200 g (7 oz) chopped walnuts	200 g (7 oz) chopped pistachios	200 g (7 oz) chopped almonds
Fruit juice	100 ml (3.5 fl oz) orange juice	100 ml (3.5 fl oz) orange juice	100 ml (3.5 fl oz) orange juice	100 ml (3.5 fl oz) raspberry purée
Liqueur	50 ml (4 tbls) Kirsch	50 ml (4 tbls) Kirsch	50 ml (4 tbls) Kirsch	50 ml (4 tbls) raspberry liqueur
Flour	50 g (1 2/3 oz)	50 g (1 2/3 oz)	50 g (1 2/3 oz)	50 g (1 2/3 oz)

C - Assembling a dome-shaped dessert

Lining the mold with fruit: Orange Dome

Line the dome-shaped mold with poached slices of orange cut in half and chilled in the freezer a few minutes.
Fill with bavarian cream and place a round of cake on top, chill until firm in the freezer.

Lining the mold with ice cream: Praline Dome

Spread firm ice cream in an even layer on the sides of the mold, leaving a space in the center. Fill with a complimentary ice cream or parfait and place in the freezer until firm.

D - Assembling a dessert in a rectangular form with a chocolate base

Spread tempered covering chocolate on the cake (cut to fit the bottomless mold). Place a sheet of parchment on top of the chocolate then invert on to the work surface. Place the mold to fit around the cake and brush with flavored syrup. Add filliing, smooth the top and chill until firm.

E - Assembling a log-shaped (bûche) dessert

Lining a bûche mold with fruits

Line the log-shaped mold with plastic wrap. Cover the inside of the mold with poached orange slices and chill. Fill with orange bavarian cream, place a rectangle of sponge cake on top and chill until firm in the freezer.

Lining a bûche mold with cake

Line the inside of the log-shaped mold with a sheet of sponge cake and brush with syrup. Fill with mousse, place a sheet of sponge cake on top and chill until firm in the freezer.

F - Shaping with a pastry bag (chestnut mice, coffee ice cream with nougatine)

The mixtures need to be cold enough to hold their shape but soft enough to flow easily from the pastry bag.

G - Shaping a mixture with a spoon («croustillants» with red fruits)

The cream should be very smooth and the spoonful should not be too large.

Post script

Culinary professions in France, whether restaurant chef, butcher, or in the case of this book, pastry chef, are taught through an apprentice program that places young students in professional kitchens from the very start to learn from experienced chefs. The skills needed to be a chef are a combination of basic techniques and more subtle «savoir faire» that must be acquired from a master.

Acquiring technical skills with hands-on experience is always accompanied by a well organized course of study.

The apprentices divide their time at the beginning between the profession kitchen and the classroom where the math, science and social skills necessary to success in the culinary field are taught. This thorough education forms a solid base for a career as a chef.

Therefore, the chefs and the professors must not only be masters of the manual skills of the trade but be good teachers as well with a desire and ability to share their knowledge. They must inspire confidence in their students and teach them the discipline to do their best.

Chef Philippe Durand with the support of Pierre Michalet, have created a teaching tool that goes beyond the classroom and profession kitchen. This beautiful book will provide culinary students as well as the general public with the information needed to learn the demanding skills of pastry making, and in particular individual desserts. Many cooks will savor the knowledge found in this book.

L. KLUCIK
Proviseur
du lycée «Louis-Guilloux» (Rennes)

Note from the editor

The production of this book was possible due to the talents and cooperation of a talented and generous team. Thanks go first and foremost to the author, Philippe Durand, who not only shared his innovative ideas for «designer desserts» but his teaching experience as well which is evident in the clear and informative text that accompanies the recipes.

Chef Durand worked long hard hours with his colleagues and students for a year to produce the stunning desserts photographed in this book. We were very fortunate to work together at the well equipped Lycée Louis Guilloux in Rennes.

Our thanks to everyone who made this book possible.

Pierre MICHALET
Editor

Photography Credits
The photographs in this book
were taken by Pierre MICHALET

Watercolors

The watercolors that illustrate the introduction to each chapter were created especially for this book by Bernadette Maes-Sarazin. This well known artist works in many medium at «Centre Ouest de la France» in St-Jean-d'Angely.

Translation

Translator Anne Sterling is a graduate and the former director of LaVarenne Ecole de Cuisine with over two decades of culinary experience. She is a food columnist, recipe consultant and teaches cooking to adults and children.

WILEY

ISBN 0-471-16064-4

John Wiley & Sons, Inc.
Professional, Reference and Trade Group
605 Third Avenue, New York, N.Y. 10158-0012
New York • Chichester • Brisbane • Toronto • Singapore

CICEM S.A.
36, rue St-Louis-en-l'Ile
75004 PARIS

ISBN 2-86871-002-6

Dépôt Légal 2ᵉ Tr. 96
Photogravure : FOTIMPRIM (Paris)
Photocomposition : BOA (Paris)
Impression : QUEBECOR (La Loupe 28)
Reliure : SIRC (Marigny-Le-Châtel 10)